BIG

SECONDGRADE
WORKBOOK
ALL SUPJECT

SKILL AREAS INCLUDE
Vocabulary – Writing – Reading Comprehension – Math – Cursive Handwriting
Word Problems – Science – Phonics – Cursive Handwriting – And More !

EMAIL US AT

scholasticzone@gmail.com

TO GET FREE GOODIES!

Just title the email

"Big Second Grade Workbook - Ages 7 to 8FREE Worksheets"

And we'll send you some extra worksheets for your kiddo!!

This Book
Belongs To:

_____

Get Ready For
Second Grade

2nd GRADE

The three bears found Goldilocks in Baby bear's bed. They were upset.

The three bears left their house and went for a walk.

...d wanted to ...'s bed was

I went on a **walk** today.

r o b e

Alex woke up and looked outside, it was very sunny and clear!

Name: _____

Long - - - - - - ➤ Or - - - - - ➤ Short

Look at the picture at the beginning of each row and say the name of
the picture. Listen for the vowel sound. Then circle the word in each row
that has the same vowel sound as the picture.

1.		bug	red	sand	table
2.		hat	book	ham	baby
3.		tan	clue	block	eye
4.		in	eye	blue	dog
5.		flower	drain	cat	food
6.		hand	on	rain	bell
7.		ten	teeth	horse	ran
8.		bed	road	fan	tree

Name: _____

Find → The → Long Vowel

Find the words in each row that has the same vowel sound.

1. Long A	cake bat rat rake
2. Long E	bread tree web knee
3. Long I	lion milk kite lips
4. Long O	dog rose snow mop
5. Long U	umbrella unicorn unicycle bug

Name: _____

Look at the pictures below. Fill in the missing vowel and the silent "e" for each word.

l __ k __	t __ __ __	r __ b __ __
m __ n __ __	t __ p __	r __ k
c __ p __ __	pl __ t __	sl __ d

Tricky  →"Y"

The letter Y can sometimes make different sounds. The "y" in puppy makes the long "e" sound, and the "y" in fly makes the long "i" sound. Look at each picture below. If it ends like puppy, write an "e" on the line. If it ends like fly, write an "i" on the line.

spy

crybaby

key

pony

honey

monkey

sky

butterfly

Name: _____

Missing - - - → Sight - - - ▸ words!

Read the sightword in each firefly. Then use each of the sightwords to complete the sentences.

really

walk

some

are

they

first

said

again

1. I went on a _____ today.

2. Do _____ want to play?

3. Can you come _____ me?

4. Can I swing_____?

5. I _____ an ice cream cone.

6. She _____ there was more dessert.

7. Can you _____ play?

8. I _____ to build things.

9. Let's do it _____!

10. What _____ that sound?

11. You _____ a good friend.

12. _____ your dog like treats?

13. I _____ like trucks!

14. Can I have _____ more cake?

does

with

was

want

come

like

Name: _____

Time To Rhyme!

Read each of the words in the box. Match each of the words in the box to the word it rhymes with below,

jump	boy	duck	boat	rock
box	bee	king	hand	fish

1. wish _____

2. sand _____

3. ring _____

4. three _____

5. fox _____

6. sock _____

7. goat _____

8. truck _____

9. toy _____

10. stump _____

Name: _____

Blend ⟶ It! ⟶ ▲

Finish each word using the correct consonant blend.

1. __ __ ail

6. __ __ im

2. __ __ etzel

7. __ __ ide

3. __ __ ink

8. __ __ ee

dr	sn
sl	tw
pr	sw
tr	sm

4. __ __ oth

9. __ __ ins

11. __ __ ess

5. __ __ ig

10. __ __ um

12. __ __ actor

Name: _____

Color the compound words yellow and the other words green.
A compound word is made of two words joined together. Example: butterfly (butter + fly).

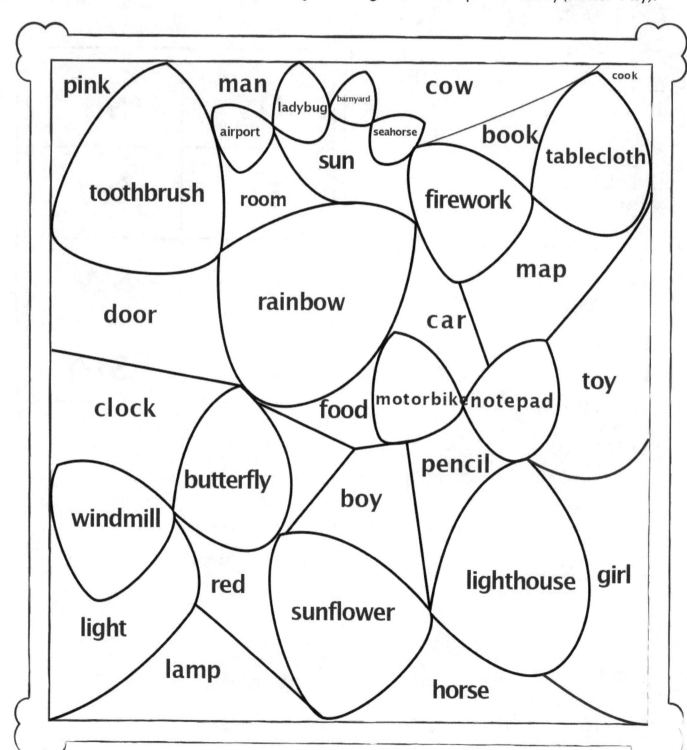

pink   man   cow   cook

ladybug   barnyard

airport   seahorse   book   tablecloth

sun

toothbrush   room   firework

map

door   rainbow   car

clock   food   motorbike notepad   toy

pencil

butterfly   boy

windmill

red   lighthouse   girl

light   sunflower

lamp   horse

Digraph → Blending

Look at the digraph. Then read the rest of the word. Write the whole word together. Reread the word.

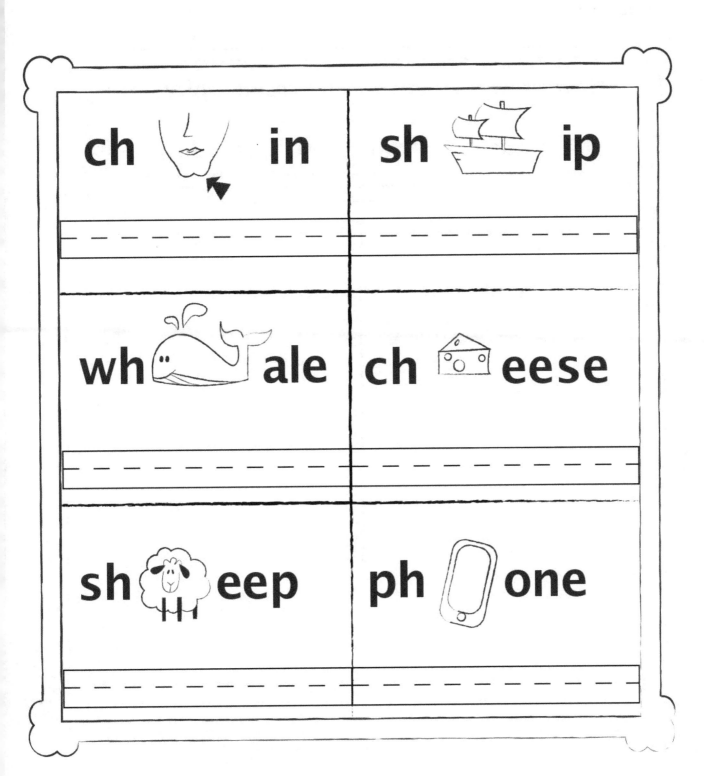

ch [image] in   sh [image] ip

wh [image] ale   ch [image] eese

sh [image] eep   ph [image] one

Name: _____

Sort - - - - → The - - - - ▸ Dipthong

Read the words in the word box. Then write the –aw words and the short–o words from the word box in the correct column.

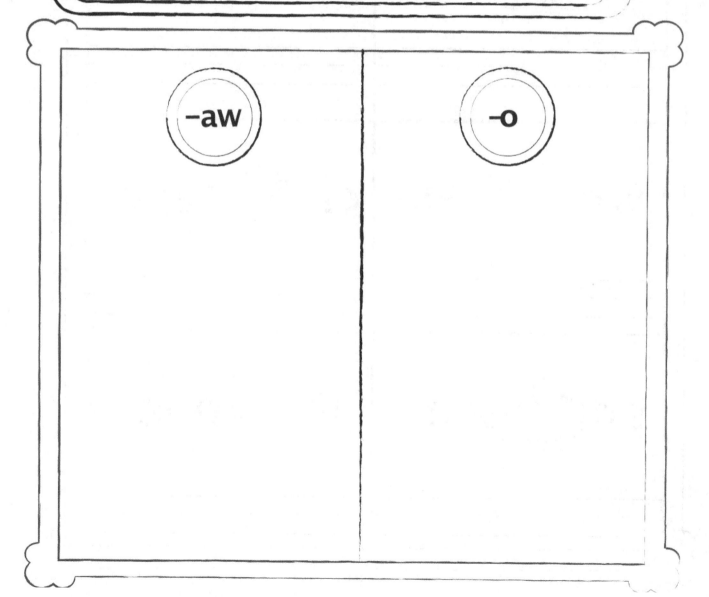

flaw   mop   fawn   jog   crawl   plop

draw   sock   straw   hop   jaw   fog

–aw

-o

Fancy ----→ Plurals ----→

Some nouns have a special plural form.

Look at each picture and use it to help you choose which plural noun to write.

One	More Than One
leaf	leaves
shelf	shelves
calf	calves
watch	watches
goose	geese

1. Look at the _____ on the tree! | leaf |

2. How many _____ are there in the kitchen? | shelf |

3. The cow had two _____ this morning. | calf |

4. How many _____ are there to choose from? | watch |

5. The _____ are flying south for the winter.
| goose |

Name: _____

 **Which** → **One?** ⤏

Finish each word by writing either **ou** or **ow**. Look at the pictures for clues.

1. fr __ __ n   2. __ __ l   3. p __ __ c h   4. f l __ __ e r

brown

5. r __ __ n d   6. b r __ __ n   7. m __ __ t h   8. s n __ __

 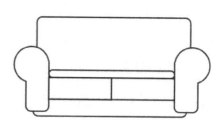

9. c r __ __ n   10. c __ __ c h

Name: _____

Honeycomb ---→ Numbers ---→

Benny the Bee is filling another honeycomb with numbers! Can you help him by filling in the missing numbers?

1	2	( )	4	5	6	7	( )	9	10
11	( )	13	14	15	16	( )	( )	19	20
21	( )	23	24	( )	( )	27	28	29	30
31	32	( )	34	35	( )	37	38	( )	40
( )	42	43	44	45	46	( )	48	49	( )
( )	52	53	54	55	56	57	58	59	60
61	( )	63	64	( )	66	67	68	69	( )
71	72	73	( )	75	76	( )	( )	79	80
( )	( )	83	84	85	86	87	88	( )	( )
91	92	93	94	95	96	( )	( )	99	100

Name: _____

Vegetable  →Math

Look at each problem. Write the equation and add the numbers to find the solutions.

1. Abby planted 9 .

    Ella gave her 10 more .

    How many are there in all?

    _____ + _____ = _____

2. Andrew planted 12 .

    Then he planted 8 more .

    How many are there in all?

    _____ + _____ = _____

3. Sara planted 10 .

    Ann gave her 7 more .

    How many  are there in all?

    _____ + _____ = _____

4. Evan planted 8 .

    Then he planted 7 more .

    How many are there in all?

    _____ + _____ = _____

Fun → With → Place Value

Look at each picture. Count the tens and the ones and then write the matching numbers in the boxes below.

Look at the example of place value here. Place value is how we describe the position of each digit in a number.

Tens — 2

Ones — 7

2 Tens 7 Ones = 27

Tens — — —

Ones — — —

[ ] Tens [ ] Ones = [— — —]

Tens — — —

Ones — — —

[ ] Tens [ ] Ones = [— — —]

Tens — — —

Ones — — —

[ ] Tens [ ] Ones = [— — —]

Tens — — —

Ones — — —

[ ] Tens [ ] Ones = [— — —]

Tens — — —

Ones — — —

[ ] Tens [ ] Ones = [— — —]

Name: _____

Add All Three

Look at the example below. Read each of the questions and solve the problem. Make sure to show your work!

Example:
At the zoo there were 4 hummingbirds, 3 finches, and 2 parrots. How many birds were there altogther?

$$4 + 3 + 2 = 9$$

1. At the beach there were 3 pink shells, 5 blue shells, and 2 yellow shells. How many shells were there altogether?

2. While driving, Sam saw 2 blue cars, 3 red cars, and 4 yellow cars. How many cars did he see altogether?

3. At the apple orchard Alice picked 4 apples, her brother picked 2 apples, and her mom picked 5 apples. How many apples did they pick altogether?

4. Adam planted 6 beans, Sue planted 5 beans, and Alex planted 2 beans. How many beans did they plant altogether?

Name: _____

Subtraction — Watermelons

Subtract the numbers inside each watermelon and circle the ones that match up to the number on the top.

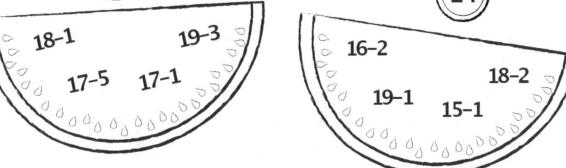

(15)

20–5

10–1

11–2

19–4

(17)

14–2

19–2

18–1

16–3

(19)

20–1

19–0

18–5

16–3

(16)

18–1

19–3

17–5

17–1

(14)

16–2

18–2

19–1

15–1

Name: _____

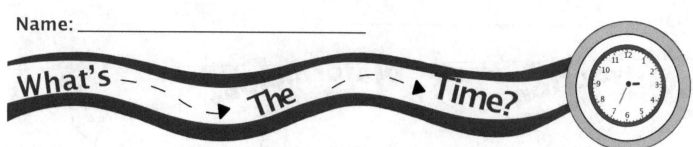

What's The Time?

Write the correct time under each clock in the first section. The first one has been done for you.

8:00

Fill in the hands on the analog clock faces to match the digital time shown. The first one has been done for you.

11:00   1:00   6:00   4:00

2:00   12:00   3:00   5:00

Name: _____

Funny ----→ Clock --- --▸ Faces

Write the time each clock shows on the lines below each clock.

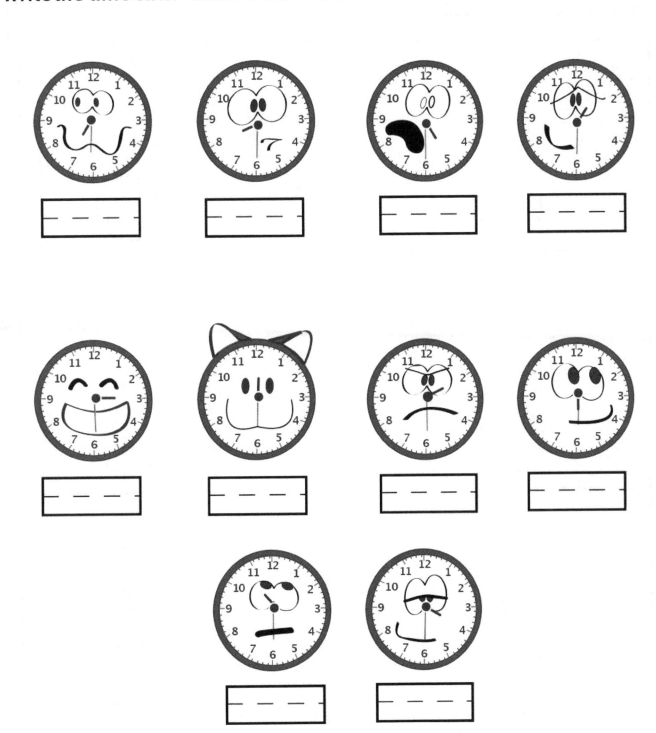

Name: _____

Ordering - - - ▶ by - - - ▶ Length

Number each set of three items from 1 to 3, 1 being the shortest and 3 being the longest.

Name: _____

Measuring ➔ Snakes

Estimate how many inches long you think each snake is from head to tail. Go back to the top of the page and use the ruler to see how close your guesses are! Record your measurement under each snake.

1	2	3	4	5	6	7

Estimated length: _____   Actual length: _____

Estimated length: _____   Actual length: _____

Estimated length: _____   Actual length: _____

Estimated length: _____   Actual length: _____

Name: _____

Tally → It → Up!

Help Ali record how many fruits and vegetables she bought at the grocery store. First, count how many of each type of fruit or vegetable she bought and mark it in the table. Then, write it in number form. Finally, answer the questions.

Type of food		Tally Marks	Number
	Broccoli		
	Carrot		
	Apple		
	Banana		

1. What fruit or vegetable does Ali have the most of?

_____

_____

2. What fruit or vegetable does Ali have the least of?

_____

_____

3. How many fruits and vegetables does Ali have in all?

_____

_____

Name: _____

Use the picture to answer the questions below.

1. How many rectangles are there?

_____

- - - - - - - - - - - - - - - -

2. How many triangles are there?

_____

- - - - - - - - - - - - - - - -

3. How many circles are there?

_____

- - - - - - - - - - - - - - - -

4. Draw 2 more rectangles and 4 more triangles in the picture.

Name: _____

Odd - - - → Number - - - ▸Gold!

Help the leprechaun find the gold at the end of the rainbow by coloring the spaces with odd numbers to show your path.

4	1	8	22	98	34	10	6	12
14	3	5	7	26	44	62	78	40
50	20	28	9	32	16	90	48	52
12	15	13	11	38	42	56	78	82
12	17	19	21	23	25	27	29	22
20	34	42	68	70	94	46	31	54
56	48	92	24	6	37	35	33	8
18	94	72	46	36	39	34	22	10

The Velveteen Rabbit Rebus Story

Name: _____   **Date:** _____

A rebus story is told using pictures and drawings instead of
words. The drawings can symbolize a sound, word or character.
Use the drawings below to fill in the blanks for a passage from
The Velveteen Rabbit by Margery Williams

Directions:

Use a pair of ✂ to cut out the pictures and then ⬛ them

onto the correct spots in the story on page 2.

The Velveteen Rabbit Rebus Story

Name: _____   Date: _____

There was once a velveteen [ ], and in

the beginning he was really splendid. He

was fat and bunchy, as a [ ] should be;

his coat was spotted [ ], he had real

thread [ ], and his [ ], were lined

with pink sateen. On Christmas morning,

when he sat wedged in the top of the

The Velveteen Rabbit Rebus Story

Boy's [ ], with a sprig of holly between

his [ ], the effect was charming. There

were other things in the stocking, nuts and

[ ] and a toy engine, and chocolate

almonds and a clockwork mouse, but the

[ ] was quite the best of all.

Picture Clues

Name: _____   **Date:** _____

Use the illustrations to describe what is happening in each picture. Color in the bubble next to the correct answer.

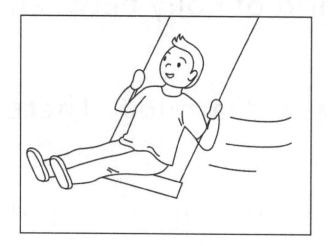

- ◯ The boy is running.
- ◯ The boy is swinging.
- ◯ The boy is crying.

- ◯ The kids are swimming.
- ◯ The kids are sliding.
- ◯ The kids are biking.

- ◯ The girl is building.
- ◯ The girl is running.
- ◯ The girl is dancing.

- ◯ The kids are dancing.
- ◯ The kids are driving.
- ◯ The kids are sleeping.

Goldilocks and the Three Bears Storyboard

Name: _____   **Date:** _____

The story is mixed up! Look at the pictures and read the words to put the story back in order again.

Bonus Activity: Color in Goldilocks and the Three Bears.

The three bears came home and saw their house was a mess!

Goldilocks woke up and saw the three bears looking at her. She ran away and won't bother them again!

The three bears found Goldilocks in Baby bear's bed. They were upset.

Goldilocks explored the three bears house and tried some porridge. Baby bear's porridge was just right.

The three bears left their house and went for a walk.

Goldilocks was tired and wanted to take a rest. Baby bear's bed was perfect.

Create a Story Map

Name: _____   **Date:** _____

Read the story. Fill in the story map using the story to help you.

Once there was a pirate ship sailing in search of treasure. They searched and searched, but didn't find any treasure. One day the captain spotted a distant island and decided to explore it. The crew sailed to the island and searched every corner. Suddenly, they spotted a chest full of gold and silver! The crew celebrated.

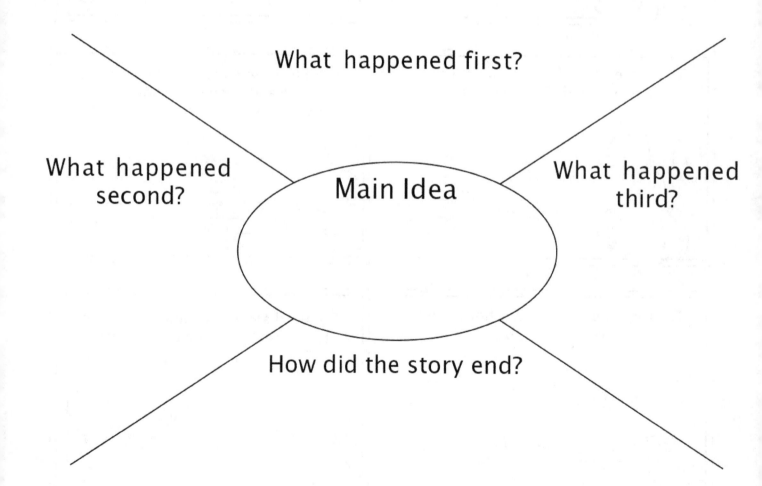

What happened first?

What happened second?

Main Idea

What happened third?

How did the story end?

Story Sequencing

Name: _____   **Date:** _____

Look at each group of pictures and decide what happened. Fill in the bubble next to the best answer.

○ The sun was shining on the farm.

○ The farmer planted seeds and the seeds grew into plants.

○ The farm is a fun place to work.

○ The kids got out their bikes and went for a ride.

○ The bikes were broken and the kids were sad.

○ The kids were looking for their bikes.

○ The boy and his dad are playing a game outside.

○ The boy is eating a cake.

○ The boy and his dad are making a cake.

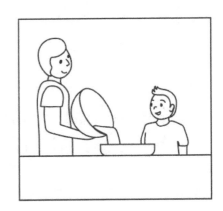

Which is it?

Name: _____ **Date:** _____

Read each sentence and decide if it is fiction or nonfiction. Cut the sentences out and glue them on the correct page.

FICTION

NONFICTION

A horse is an animal with four legs.

The spider and the fly were friends who loved to play tag.

"I'm flying!" Ella said as she jumped off her bed.

Rain is an important part of the water cycle.

Main Idea: Farmers

Name: _____   **Date:** _____

Read each sentence. Cut the sentences out and decide which sentence is the main idea and which are the supporting details. Glue the sentences in order in the boxes provided.

Main Idea:

Supporting Detail 1

Supporting Detail 2

Supporting Detail 3

Farmers grow vegetables that people buy and eat.

Farmers plant vegetable seeds in the fields.

Farmers harvest the vegetable plants.

People buy the vegetables and eat them.

Exploring a Table of Contents

Name: _____   **Date:** _____

Use the table of contents to answer the questions below.

1. How many chapters are in this book? _____

2. What page would you turn to if you wanted to learn about sculptures? _____

3. If you opened the book to page 56, what type of project would you learn about? _____

4. How many types of painting can you learn about in this book? _____

5. What page would you turn to in order to learn more about the author? _____

6. On what page can you learn how to make dolls? _____

7. What is Chapter 2 about? _____

8. What page would you turn to find the index? _____

9. On what page can you learn about finger painting? _____

Finish the Fact Cloud

Name: _____   **Date:** _____

Use the blank fact bubbles to record four new facts you learned
as you read a book.

Inference Puzzles

Name: _____   **Date:** _____

Look at each picture. Circle your best guess using the picture clues.

The boy is painting.

The boy has finished painting and is cleaning up his supplies.

The farmer is harvesting vegetables.

The farmer is planting seeds.

The girl is going for a bike ride.

The girl has finished riding her bike.

The man is making dinner.

The man is eating dinner.

The girl is putting her blocks away.

The girl is building with her blocks.

Choose the Best Ending

Name: _____   **Date:** _____

Look at each picture. Read the beginning of each story and choose which sentence best finishes the story. Circle the best ending.

Alex woke up and looked outside, it was very sunny and clear! She was so excited to meet her friend Susan to play in the park. She decided to put on...

1. her sun hat and sandals.

2. her heavy coat, mittens, and boots.

Sam was making a cake for his brother's birthday. He started by looking at the recipe and getting out all of his ingredients and supplies. Then he began....

1. to mix the ingredients one at a time.

2. to decorate the cake for the party.

The pilot got the plane ready for take off. He checked all of the instruments and told his crew to buckle in. Then he....

1. started to lift the plane off the ground.

2. landed the plane on the runway.

Connect It

Read the story and use the questions at the bottom to make connections to things in your real life.

It was the last day of school and Eliza was so excited about summer break! She said goodbye to Ms. B and ran to her mom with a bag full of her art projects from 1st grade. Her mom said, "Do you want to get an ice cream cone to celebrate summer break?" She jumped up and down and said, "Yes!" loudly. Eliza started to think about all of the fun she was going to have this summer. It was going to be a great summer!

Match the beginning of each sentence to the ending that makes the most sense. Draw a line or fill in the blank with a letter.

1) This story reminds me of myself because _____

a) I feel excited about summer break.

2) This story reminds me of a book I read because _____

b) There are so many things to do during summer break.

3) This story reminds me of the real world because _____

c) It is about the last day of first grade.

Finish that Sentence!

Name:_____ Date:_____

Finish the sentences to write a story.

1. Who?

The dog

2. What?

The dog is going

3. Where?

4. Why?

5. When?

Silly Story Starter

Name:_____   Date:_____

Look at the picture below. Write a story about this picture. What happened?

_____

_____

_____

_____

_____

_____

_____

Tell a Story: Summer Adventure

Name:_____   Date:_____

Look at the scene below. Write a story about the scene
using as many details as you can. Use your imagination!
When you finish, color the scene.

Sight Word Sentences

Name:_____ Date:_____

Use the sight words to write four different sentences on the lines below. Use at least one sight word in each sentence.

Them Why   Could
Do

Writing Questions: Summer

Name:_____   Date:_____

Finish each sentence by filling in the first word using a word from the word bank, and end the sentence with a question mark.

1. _____ is your birthday___

2. _____ you like to swim___

3. _____ is your favorite flavor of ice cream___

4. _____ it hot outside today___

5. _____ we go to the beach___

6. _____ you happy it is summer___

When, Do, What, Is, Should, Are

Find the Fact!

Name:_____ Date:_____

Choose a nonfiction book to read. Find three facts from the book. Then, draw a picture for each fact and write a caption for each picture.

Fact:_____

_____

_____

Caption:_____

Fact:_____

_____

_____

Caption:_____

Fact:_____

_____

_____

Caption:_____

Sentence Practice

Name:_____ Date:_____

Did you know that there are three major kinds of sentences?
Declarative: a sentence that makes a statement.
Exclamatory: a sentence that expresses a strong feeling.
Interrogative: a sentence that asks a question.

Use the pictures on each line to help you write a declarative, exclamatory, or interrogative sentence. Don't forget to punctuate!

Write a declarative sentence.

Dogs like to play.

Write an exclamatory sentence.

Write an interrogative sentence.

Write a declarative sentence.

Write an exclamatory sentence.

Write an interrogative sentence.

Finish the Story!

Name:_____   Date:_____

Read the story. Finish the story using the empty boxes below.

Beginning: Alice and her dog Bobo were going to play fetch at the park. Bobo loved to play fetch and Alice had been teaching him different tricks all summer. She couldn't wait to show her friends what he could do!

Middle 1: Alice unclipped Bobo's leash and threw the ball. Bobo ran after the ball and caught it while it was still in the air!

Middle 3: Alice was so worried about Bobo, she hoped he would come back soon.

Middle 2:

Ending:

Fix the Sentences: Pets

Name:_____ Date:_____

Oh no! The sentences are written incorrectly. Rewrite
each sentence to fix it.

the dog plays.

fish is swimming. The

the hamster runs

horse The eats.

All About Butterflies

Name:_____   Date:_____

Look at the picture and fill in the blanks using the words at the bottom of the page.

Forewing

Clubbed Antenna

Head

Compound Eye

Proboscis

Abdomen

T h o r a x L e g s

Butterfliesareakindof_____that

have compound_____, six_____, and

two_____ onthetopof theirhead.

Theyhavecolorful_____ and a longstraw-

liketonguecalleda_____.

---

insect, legs, wings, antennae, proboscis, eyes

Read, Write, and Draw: Summer

Name:_____   Date:_____

Summer is the warmest season of the year, between spring and fall. In summer, the nights are shortest and days are longest.

Draw yourself all dressed up for warm weather.

Draw your favorite summer activity.

How do you celebrate holidays in summer?

_____

_____

_____

_____

_____

Punctuation: At the Beach

Name:_____ Date:_____

Finish each sentence by writing a question mark, exclamation mark, or period.

I love to swim____

Did you see that turtle____

Wow, that is the biggest sand castle____

Do you know where the shovel is____

I'm going to make a mermaid in the sand____

Can we get ice cream after lunch____

That surfer went up really high____

Are dogs allowed on the beach____

Answer Sheets

Get Ready for Second Grade

Is It Long or Short?
Find the Long Vowel
Finish the Silent E Words
Tricky Y
Missing Sight Words
Find That Rhyme
Blending Consonants
Color the Compound Words
Digraph Blending
Sort the Diphthong
Fancy Plurals
Which Diphthong?
Honey Comb Numbers
Vegetable Math
Fun With Place Value
Add All Three
Subtraction Watermelons
What is the Time?
Funny Clock Faces
Measuring Snakes
Tally It Up at the Grocery Store!
Shape Pictures: Space Travel
Odd Number Gold

Velveteen Rabbit Rebus Story
Picture Clues
Goldilocks and the Three Bears Storyboard
Create a Story Map
Story Sequencing
Which Is It?
Main Idea: Farmers
Exploring a Table of Contents
Inference Puzzles
Choose the Best Ending
Writing Questions: Summer
Fix the Sentences: Pets
All About Butterflies
Punctuation: At the Beach

Answer Sheet

Name: _____

Long ----- ➤ Or -----➤ Short

Look at the picture at the beginning of each row and say the name of the picture. Listen for the vowel sound. Then circle the word in each row that has the same vowel sound as the picture.

ANSWER SHEET

#	Picture	Words
1.		bug (red) sand table
2.		(hat) book ham baby
3.		tan (clue) block eye
4		in eye (blue) dog
5.		flower (drain) cat food
6.		hand (on) rain bell
7.		ten (teeth) horse ran
8.		bed (road) fan tree

Answer Sheet

Name: _____

Find → The → Long Vowel

Find the words in each row that has the same vowel sound.

ANSWER SHEET

1. Long A	(cake)　bat　rat　(rake)
2. Long E	bread　(tree)　web　(knee)
3. Long I	(lion)　milk　(kite)　lips
4. Long O	dog　(rose)　(snow)　mop
5. Long U	umbrella　(unicorn)　(unicycle)　bug

Answer Sheet

Name: _____

Finish **The** **Silent** **"E"**

Look at the pictures below. Fill in the missing vowel and the silent "e" for each word.

ANSWER SHEET

lake	tie	robe
mane	tape	rake
cape	plate	slide

Answer Sheet

Name: _____

Tricky → "Y" →

The letter Y can sometimes make different sounds. The "y" in puppy makes the long "e" sound, and the "y" in fly makes the long "i" sound. Look at each picture below. If it ends like puppy, write an "e" on the line. If it ends like fly, write an "i" on the line.

ANSWER SHEET

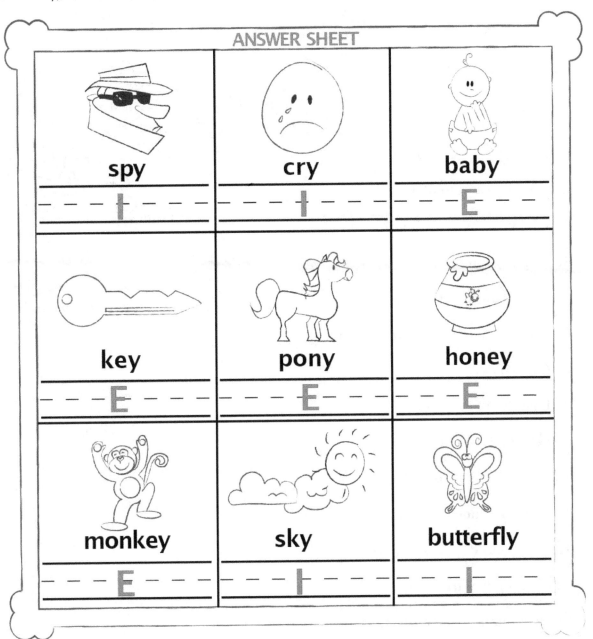

Answer Sheet

Missing - - - → Sight - - - ▶ words!

Read the sightword in each firefly. Then use each of the sightwords to complete the sentences.

ANSWER SHEET

1. I went on a walk today.

2. Do they want to play?

3. Can you come with me?

4. Can I swing first?

5. I want an ice cream cone.

6. She said there was more dessert.

7. Can you come play?

8. I like to build things.

9. Let's do it again!

10. What was that sound?

11. You are a good friend.

12. Does your dog like treats?

13. I really like trucks!

14. Can I have some more cake?

Answer Sheet

Name: _____

Time → To → Rhyme!

Read each of the words in the box. Match each of the words in the box to the word it rhymes with below.

ANSWER SHEET

jump	boy	duck	boat	rock
box	bee	king	hand	fish

1. wish   fish

2. sand   hand

3. ring   king

4. three   bee

5. fox   box

6. sock   rock

7. goat   boat

8. truck   duck

9. toy   boy

10. stump jump

Answer Sheet

Name: _____

Blend ➤ It!

Finish each word using the correct consonant blend.

1. snail

6. swim

2. pretzel

7. slide

3. drink

8. tree

Answer Sheet

dr	sn
sl	tw
pr	sw
tr	sm

4. sloth

9. twins

11. dress

5. twig

10. drum

12. tractor

Answer Sheet

ANSWER SHEET

Name: _____

Color → The → Compound Words

Color the compound words yellow and the other words green.
A compound word is made of two words joined together. Example: butterfly (butter + fly).

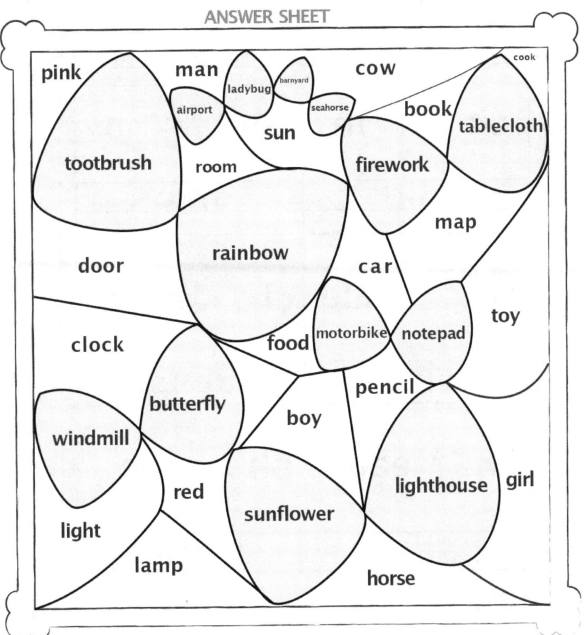

pink   man   cow   cook
ladybug   barnyard
airport   seahorse   book   tablecloth
sun
tootbrush   room   firework
map
door   rainbow   car
toy
clock   food   motorbike   notepad
pencil
butterfly   boy
windmill   lighthouse   girl
red
light   sunflower
lamp   horse

Answer Sheet

Look at the digraph. Then read the rest of the word. Write the whole word together. Reread the word.

ANSWER SHEET

ch [face] in	sh [ship] ip
chin	ship
wh [whale] ale	ch [cheese] eese
whale	cheese
sh [sheep] eep	ph [phone] one
sheep	phone

Answer Sheet

Name: _____

Sort → The → Dipthong

Read the words in the word box. Then write the -aw words and the short-o words from the word box in the correct column.

ANSWER SHEET

flaw   mop   fawn   jog   crawl   plop

draw   sock   straw   hop   jaw   fog

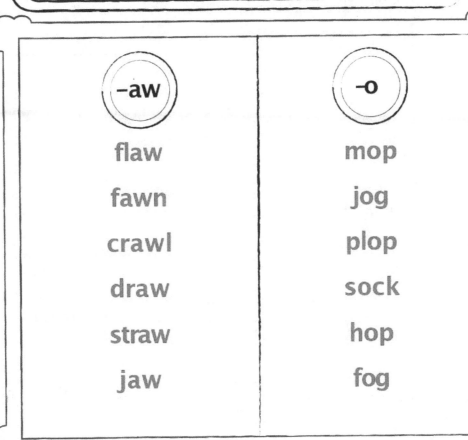

-aw	-o
flaw	mop
fawn	jog
crawl	plop
draw	sock
straw	hop
jaw	fog

Answer Sheet

 **Fancy → Plurals**

ANSWER SHEET

Some nouns have a special plural form.

Look at each picture and use it to help you choose which plural noun to write.

One	More Than One
leaf	leaves
shelf	shelves
calf	calves
watch	watches
goose	geese

 1. Look at the ___leaves___ on the tree! | leaf |

 2. How many ___shelves___ are there in the kitchen? | shelf |

 3. The cow had two ___calves___ this morning. | calf |

 4. How many ___watches___ are there to choose from? | watch |

 5. The ___geese___ are flying south for the winter. | goose |

Answer Sheet

Name: _____

Which → **One?**

Finish each word by writing either **ou** or **ow**. Look at the pictures for clues.

ANSWER SHEET

1. frown

2. owl

3. pouch

4. flower

5. round

6. brown

7. mouth

8. snow

9. crown

10. couch

Answer Sheet

Answer Sheet

Name: _____

Honeycomb - - - ► Numbers - - - ►

Benny the Bee is filling another honeycomb with numbers! Can you help him by filling in the missing numbers?

1	2	3	4	5	6	7	8	9	10
11	12	13	14	15	16	17	18	19	20
21	22	23	24	25	26	27	28	29	30
31	32	33	34	35	36	37	38	39	40
41	42	43	44	45	46	47	48	49	50
51	52	53	54	55	56	57	58	59	60
61	62	63	64	65	66	67	68	69	70
71	72	73	74	75	76	77	78	79	80
81	82	83	84	85	86	87	88	89	90
91	92	93	94	95	96	97	98	99	100

Answer Sheet

Name: _____

Vegetable ----→ Math ---- ▲

Look at each problem. Write the equation and add the numbers to find the solutions.

ANSWER SHEET

1. Abby planted 9 .

   Ella gave her 10 more .

   How many are there in all?

   $\underline{\quad 9 \quad} + \underline{\quad 10 \quad} = \underline{\quad 19 \quad}$

2. Andrew planted 12 .

   Then he planted 8 more .

   How many are there in all?

   $\underline{\quad 12 \quad} + \underline{\quad 8 \quad} = \underline{\quad 20 \quad}$

3. Sara planted 10 .

   Ann gave her 7 more .

   How many are there in all?

   $\underline{\quad 10 \quad} + \underline{\quad 7 \quad} = \underline{\quad 17 \quad}$

4. Evan planted 8 .

   Then he planted 7 more.

   How many are there in all?

   $\underline{\quad 8 \quad} + \underline{\quad 7 \quad} = \underline{\quad 15 \quad}$

Answer Sheet

ANSWER SHEET

Name: _____

Fun - - → With - → Place Value

Look at each picture. Count the tens and the ones and then write the matching numbers in the boxes below.

Look at the example of place value here. Place value is how we describe the position of each digit in a number.

Tens — 2 —
Ones — 7 —

2 Tens   7 Ones = 27

Tens — 6 —
Ones — 7 —

6 Tens   7 Ones = 67

Tens — 7 —
Ones — 1 —

7 Tens   1 Ones = 71

Tens — 2 —
Ones — 3 —

2 Tens   3 Ones = 23

Tens — 4 —
Ones — 1 —

4 Tens   1 Ones = 1

4

Tens — 8 —
Ones — 8 —

8 Tens   8 Ones = 8

Answer Sheet

Name: _____

Add - - - → All - - → Three - - →

Look at the example below. Read each of the questions and solve the problem. Make sure to show your work!

Example:
At the zoo there were 4 hummingbirds, 3 finches, and 2 parrots. How many birds were there altogther?

$$4 + 3 + 2 = 9$$

1. At the beach there were 3 pink shells, 5 blue shells, and 2 yellow shells. How many shells were there altogether?

$$3 + 5 + 2 = 10$$

2. While driving, Sam saw 2 blue cars, 3 red cars, and 4 yellow cars. How many cars did he see altogether?

$$2 + 3 + 4 = 9$$

3. At the apple orchard Alice picked 4 apples, her brother picked 2 apples, and her mom picked 5 apples. How many apples did they pick altogether?

$$4 + 2 + 5 = 11$$

4. Adam planted 6 beans, Sue planted 5 beans, and Alex planted 2 beans. How many beans did they plant altogether?

$$6 + 5 + 2 = 13$$

Answer Sheet

Name: _____

Subtraction ▸ Watermelons

Subtract the numbers inside each watermelon and circle the ones that match up to the number on the top.

ANSWER SHEET

15

(20–5)
10–1
11–2 (19–4)

17

14–2 (19–2)
(18–1) 16–3

19

(20–1) (19–0)
18–5 16–3

16

18–1 (19–3)
17–5 (17–1)

14

(16–2)
18–2
19–1 (15–1)

Answer Sheet

ANSWER SHEET

Name: _____

What's → The → Time?

Write the correct time under each clock in the first section. The first one has been done for you.

8:00   5:00   3:00   12:00

2:00   6:00   11:00   4:00

Fill in the hands on the analog clock faces to match the digital time shown. The first one has been done for you.

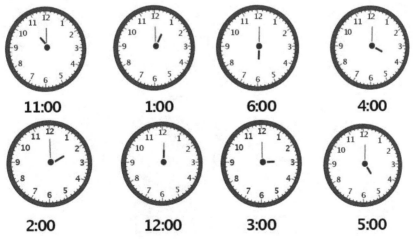

11:00   **1:00**   **6:00**   **4:00**

2:00   **12:00**   **3:00**   **5:00**

Answer Sheet

Name: _____

Funny - - - → Clock - - - ▶ Faces

Write the time each clock shows on the lines below each clock.

ANSWER SHEET

 8:30 5:30 1:30

3:30 12:30 2:30 6:30

11:30 4:30

Answer Sheet

Name: _____

Measuring → Snakes

Estimate how many inches long you think each snake is from head to tail.
Go back to the top of the page and use the ruler to see how close your
guesses are! Record your measurement under each snake.

ANSWER SHEET

Estimated length: _____   Actual length: _____ 6 _____

Estimated length: _____   Actual length: _____ 2 _____

Estimated length: _____   Actual length: _____ 3.5 _____

Estimated length: _____   Actual length: _____ 7 _____

Answer Sheet

Name: _____

Tally - - - - → It - - - → Up!

Help Ali record how many fruits and vegetables she bought at the grocery store. First, count how many of each type of fruit or vegetable she bought and mark it in the table. Then, write it in number form. Finally, answer the questions.

ANSWER SHEET

Type of food	Tally Marks	Number
Broccoli		9
Carrot		5
Apple		9
Banana		6

1. What fruit or vegetable does Ali have the most of?

Apples and Broccoli

2. What fruit or vegetable does Ali have the least of?

Carrots

3. How many fruits and vegetables does Ali have in all?

9 + 5 + 9 + 6 = 29

Answer Sheet

Name: _____

Use the picture to answer the questions below.

Answer Sheet

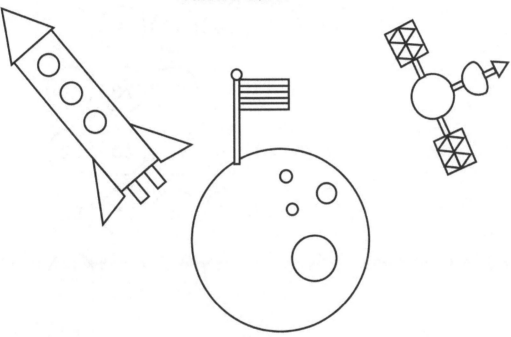

1. How many rectangles are there?

   15

2. How many triangles are there?

   12

3. How many circles are there?

   10

4. Draw 2 more rectangles and 4 more triangles in the picture.

Answer Sheet

Name: _____

Odd - - - → Number - - - ▶ Gold!

Help the leprechaun find the gold at the end of the rainbow by coloring the spaces with odd numbers to show your path. Answer Sheet

4	1	8	22	98	34	10	6	12
14	3	5	7	26	44	62	78	40
50	20	28	9	32	16	90	48	52
12	15	13	11	38	42	56	78	82
12	17	19	21	23	25	27	29	22
20	34	42	68	70	94	46	31	54
56	48	92	24	6	37	35	33	8
18	94	72	46	36	39	34	22	10

Answer Sheet

Answers
The Velveteen Rabbit Rebus Story

Name: _____ **Date:** _____

There was once a velveteen , and in

the beginning he was really splendid. He

was fat and bunchy, as a should be;

his coat was spotted , he had real

thread , and his , were lined

with pink sateen. On Christmas morning,

when he sat wedged in the top of the

Answer Sheet

The Velveteen Rabbit Rebus Story

Name: _____   **Date:** _____

Boy's [stocking] , with a sprig of holly between

his [heel] , the effect was charming. There

were other things in the stocking, nuts and

[oranges] and a toy engine, and chocolate

almonds and a clockwork mouse, but the

[rabbit] was quite the best of all.

Answer Sheet

Picture Clues

Name: _____   **Date:** _____

Use the illustrations to describe what is happening in each picture. Color in the bubble next to the correct answer.

○ The boy is running.
● The boy is swinging.
○ The boy is crying.

○ The kids are swimming.
○ The kids are sliding.
● The kids are biking.

● The girl is building.
○ The girl is running.
○ The girl is dancing.

● The kids are dancing.
○ The kids are driving.
○ The kids are sleeping.

Answer Sheet

Goldilocks and the Three Bears Storyboard

Name: _____   **Date:** _____

The story is mixed up! Look at the pictures and read the words to put the story back in order again.

Bonus Activity: Color in Goldilocks and the Three Bears.

The three bears left their house and went for a walk.

1

Goldilocks explored the three bears house and tried some porridge. Baby bear's porridge was just right.

2

MAMA   BABY   PAPA

Goldilocks was tired and wanted to take a rest. Baby bear's bed was perfect.

3

The three bears came home and saw their house was a mess!

4

The three bears found Goldilocks in Baby bear's bed. They were upset.

5

Goldilocks woke up and saw the three bears looking at her. She ran away and won't bother them again!

6

Answer Sheet

Create a Story Map

Name: _____   **Date:** _____

Read the story. Fill in the story map using the story to help you.

Once there was a pirate ship sailing in search of treasure. They searched and searched, but didn't find any treasure. One day the captain spotted a distant island and decided to explore it. The crew sailed to the island and searched every corner. Suddenly, they spotted a chest full of gold and silver! The crew celebrated.

What happened first?

A pirate ship was searching for treasure.

What happened second?

They saw an island and sailed to it.

Main Idea

A pirate ship was searching for treasure.

What happened third?

They searched the island.

How did the story end?

The crew found treasure and celebrated.

Answer Sheet

Story Sequencing

Name: _____   **Date:** _____

Look at each group of pictures and decide what happened. Fill in the bubble next to the best answer.

○ The sun was shining on the farm.

● The farmer planted seeds and the seeds grew into plants.

○ The farm is a fun place to work.

● The kids got out their bikes and went for a ride.

○ The bikes were broken and the kids were sad.

○ The kids were looking for their bikes.

○ The boy and his dad are playing a game outside.

○ The boy is eating a cake.

● The boy and his dad are making a cake.

Answer Sheet

Which is it?

Name: _____   **Date:** _____

Read each sentence and decide if it is fiction or nonfiction. Cut the sentences out and glue them on the correct page.

FICTION

A horse is an animal with four legs.

Rain is an important part of the water cycle.

NONFICTION

The spider and the fly were friends who loved to play tag.

"I'm flying!" Ella said as she jumped off her bed.

A horse is an animal with four legs.

The spider and the fly were friends who loved to play tag.

"I'm flying!" Ella said as she jumped off her bed.

Rain is an important part of the water cycle.

Answer Sheet

Main Idea: Farmers

Name: _____ **Date:** _____

Read each sentence. Cut the sentences out and decide which sentence is the main idea and which are the supporting details. Glue the sentences in order in the boxes provided.

Main Idea:

Farmers grow vegetables that people buy and eat.

Supporting Detail 1

Farmers plant vegetable seeds in the fields.

Supporting Detail 2

Farmers harvest the vegetable plants.

Supporting Detail 3

People buy the vegetables and eat them.

Farmers grow vegetables that people buy and eat.

Farmers plant vegetable seeds in the fields.

Farmers harvest the vegetable plants.

People buy the vegetables and eat them.

Answer Sheet

Exploring a Table of Contents

Name: _____   **Date:** _____

Use the table of contents to answer the questions below.

Art Projects

1. How many chapters are in this book? _____4_____

2. What page would you turn to if you wanted to learn about sculptures? _____42_____

3. If you opened the book to page 56, what type of project would you learn about? Paper airplanes

4. How many types of painting can you learn about in this book? _____3_____

5. What page would you turn to in order to learn more about the author? _____66_____

6. On what page can you learn how to make dolls? _____29_____

7. What is Chapter 2 about? _Sewing_____

8. What page would you turn to find the index? _____65_____

9. On what page can you learn about finger painting? _____20_____

Answer Sheet

Inference Puzzles

Name: _____   Date: _____

Look at each picture. Circle your best guess using the picture clues.

(The boy is painting.)

The boy has finished painting and is cleaning up his supplies.

The farmer is harvesting vegetables.

(The farmer is planting seeds.)

(The girl is going for a bike ride.)

The girl has finished riding her bike.

(The man is making dinner.)

The man is eating dinner.

The girl is putting her blocks away.

(The girl is building with her blocks.)

Answer Sheet

Choose the Best Ending

Name: _____ Date: _____

Look at each picture. Read the beginning of each story and choose which sentence best finishes the story. Circle the best ending.

Alex woke up and looked outside, it was very sunny and clear! She was so excited to meet her friend Susan to play in the park. She decided to put on...

1. her sun hat and sandals.

2. her heavy coat, mittens, and boots.

Sam was making a cake for his brother's birthday. He started by looking at the recipe and getting out all of his ingredients and supplies. Then he began....

1. to mix the ingredients one at a time.

2. to decorate the cake for the party.

The pilot got the plane ready for take off. He checked all of the instruments and told his crew to buckle in. Then he....

1. started to lift the plane off the ground.

2. landed the plane on the runway.

Writing Questions: Summer

ANSWERS

Finish each sentence by filling in the first word using a word from the word bank, and end the sentence with a question mark.

1. **When** is your birthday __

2. **Do** you like to swim __

3. **What** is your favorite flavor of ice cream __

4. **Is** it hot outside today __

5. **Should** we go to the beach __

6. **Are** you happy it is summer __

When, Do, What, Is, Should, Are

Answer Sheet

ANSWERS

Fix the Sentences: Pets

Oh no! The sentences are written incorrectly. Rewrite each sentence to fix it.

the dog plays.

The dog plays.

fish is swimming. The

The fish is swimming.

the hamster runs

The hamster runs.

horse The eats.

The horse eats.

ANSWERS All About Butterflies

Look at the picture and fill in the blanks using the words at the bottom of the page.

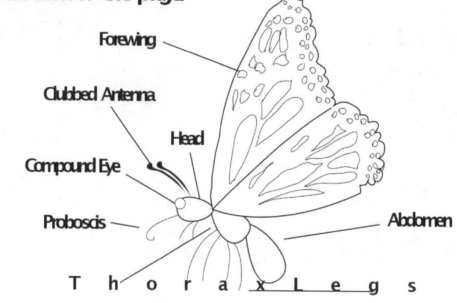

Forewing

Clubbed Antenna

Head

Compound Eye

Proboscis

Abdomen

T h o r a x L e g s

Butterflies are a kind of ____INSECT____ that

have compound ____EYES____, six ____LEGS____,

and two ____ANTENNAE____ on the top of their

head. They have colorful ____WINGS____ and a long

straw-like tongue called a ____PROBOSCIS____.

---

insect, legs, wings, antennae, proboscis, eyes

Punctuation: At the Beach

Name:_____   Date:_____

Finish each sentence by writing a question mark, exclamation mark, or period.

I love to swim _.__

Did you see that turtle_?__

Wow, that is the biggest sand castle_!__

Do you know where the shovel is_?__

I'm going to make a mermaid in the sand_.__

Can we get ice cream after lunch_?__

That surfer went up really high_!__

Are dogs allowed on the beach_?__

American Heroes
Reading Comprehension

2nd GRADE

Thomas A. Edison

Rosa Parks

Abraham Lincoln

Martin Luther King Jr.

Table of Contents

American Heroes: Reading Comprehension

Abraham Lincoln

Abraham Lincoln was the 16th President of the United States. He became President in 1861. He was President during the Civil War and helped keep the Union from splitting into two countries. In 1863, he signed the Emancipation Proclamation, the document that set all American slaves free.

Word scramble!

Unscramble the letters to form the word that completes the sentence.

1. Lincoln was born in the state of _____ . UNEKTCYK

2. Lincoln once worked as a _____ . EALYRW

3. Lincoln's wife's name was _____ . AMYR

Answers: 1. KENTUCKY   2. LAWYER   3. MARY

John Adams

John Adams

John Adams was the second President of the United States.
He was a delegate to the Continental Congress, which governed
the colonies before they became the United States of America.
Adams helped the United States become independent from Britain.

Word scramble!

Unscramble the letters to form the word that completes
the sentence.

1. Adams was also the first _____President.   IVEC

2. Adams' son, John _____ Adams, was the 6th   YUQICN
   President of the United States.

3. Adams was the only one of the first five Presidents   ELSAVS
   who did not own _____ .

Answers   1. VICE   2. QUINCY   3. SLAVES

Alexander Hamilton

Alexander Hamilton, one of America's Founding Fathers, had a key role in writing the Constitution of the United States. His ideas about government shaped the Constitution, as well as the government we have today. All of the States had to accept the Constitution before it became official, and Hamilton was mostly responsible for convincing his home state of New York to sign on. He was also the nation's first Secretary of the Treasury.

Word scramble!

Unscramble the letters to form the word that completes the sentence.

1. Hamilton fought on the side of the American colonies in the
_____ War.   IONVOLUTARYRE

2. He fought under General George _____ , who was so
impressed that he gave Hamilton a job as his aide. HINWAGTSON

3. Hamilton wanted to create a strong _____ , or national,
government for the United States.   ALEFRDE

Eleanor Roosevelt

Eleanor Roosevelt was born in 1884. She was a writer and a humanitarian, a person who works to help the poor and disadvantaged. She spoke out for human rights, equality for all, and children's causes. To help women gain equal rights in a time when they had few, President John F. Kennedy made her the leader of a special group called the Presidential Commission on the Status of Women.

Word scramble!

Unscramble the letters to form the word that completes the sentence.

1. Eleanor was also the wife of President _____ D. Roosevelt.   LIRANFNK

2. Her humanitarian work changed the way America thought about what a _____ Lady could be.   STIRF

3. Roosevelt spoke for the U.S. as a member of the _____ Nations, a group of countries from around the world who work for peace and security for all nations.   EDNIUT

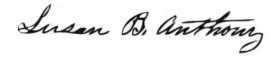

Susan B. Anthony

Susan B. Anthony was born in Massachusetts in 1820. A civil rights leader, she is best known for helping women win the right to vote in the United States. In 1872, Anthony was one of the first women ever to vote in a Presidential election in the United States. Though she did not live to see it pass, the 19th Amendment gave women the right to vote on August 18, 1920. She believed in equal rights for all people living in the United States, and she spoke out and worked against slavery.

Word scramble!

Unscramble the letters to form the word that completes the sentence.

1. The right of women to vote in elections is called women's
   _____ .

   FUAGFRSE

2. Anthony helped pass the 13th Amendment, which _____, or freed, all of the slaves.

   ATEANEMPCID

3. In the last public speech of her life, Anthony inspired those working for women's rights by saying, "Failure is _____ ."

   OSIMPBLESI

Lorraine Hansberry

Playwright and author

Lorraine Hansberry was born in Chicago, Illinois in 1930. When she was still a small child, Hansberry's family moved to a restricted neighborhood for white residents, which was against the law at the time. Hansberry's father took the family's case all the way to the Supreme Court, and her mother stayed to guard the home, ready to defend her children if necessary. The family won their case, but the experience affected Hansberry deeply. Her best-known work, a dramatic play called <u>A Raisin in the Sun</u>, was inspired by these events. It was the first play written by an African-American to be produced on Broadway. At the age of 29, Hansberry became the youngest American playwright to receive the prestigious New York Drama Critics Circle Award for Best Play. Hansberry's promising career was cut short by her death from pancreatic cancer at the age of 34.

Word scramble!

Unscramble the letters to form the word that completes the sentence.

1. <u>A Raisin in the Sun</u> was also the first play on Broadway with an African-American _____ , Lloyd Richards.   TORREDIC

2. The 1961 film version of <u>A Raisin in the Sun</u> starred legendary African-American actor Sydney _____ .   OIIEPTR

3. A 2004 Broadway revival of <u>A Raisin in the Sun</u>, starring Sean "_____" Combs, received a Tony Award nomination for Best Revival of a Play.   YIDDD

Answers: 1 DIRECTOR   2 POITIER   3 DIDDY

Maya Angelou

Writer,
producer,
performer,
professor

Maya Angelou was born in St. Louis, Missouri in 1928. As a young woman, she joined Martin Luther King, Jr. and other leaders to establish Civil Rights organizations and work for equality for African-Americans. She was devastated when King was assassinated on April 4, 1968, which also happened to be her birthday. To begin dealing with her grief, she wrote the first of six autobiographical volumes, I Know Why the Caged Bird Sings. The book won international acclaim, and she went on to become a successful writer, producer, actor and teacher. In 2010, President Barack Obama announced that Angelou would receive the Presidential Medal of Freedom, the highest civilian award in the United States.

Word scramble!

Unscramble the letters to form the word that completes the sentence.

1. Angelou is a highly trained dancer who studied and performed with famed African-American choreographer Alvin _____ .

   EYILA

2. One of her books of poetry, Just Give Me a Cool Drink of Water 'Fore I Diiiie, was nominated for a _____ Prize.

   ZEULIRPT

3. Angelou recited her poem, "On the Pulse of Morning," at the _____ ceremony for President Bill Clinton.

   TIOAUNINRAGU

Answers: 1. AILEY 2. PULITZER 3. INAUGURATION

Celia Cruz

Celia Cruz was born in Cuba, and became a citizen of the United States in 1959. She was a well-known singer of salsa songs, and introduced Cuban music to the people of the United States. She won seven Grammy Awards, the most important awards in American music. She received the National Medal of the Arts award in 1994.

Word scramble!

Unscramble the letters to form the word that completes the sentence.

1. Cruz recorded albums with some of the most famous musicians in _____ music. NLIAT

2. "Salsa" is not only the name for a kind of music, but also for a kind of _____ . ACEDN

3. Cuba is an island nation in a part of the ocean called the _____ Sea. EANACBRIB

Answers 1. LATIN 2. DANCE 3. CARIBBEAN

Rosa Parks

In 1955, one woman's refusal to give up her seat on a bus helped end segretation on public buses. That woman was Rosa Parks, and when she disobeyed a bus driver who ordered her to give her seat to a white passenger, she was arrested and taken to jail. Though other African-Americans had bravely refused to give up their seats on buses in the past, it was the Montgomery Bus Boycott, led in part by Rosa Parks, that helped end segregation on public transportation.

Word scramble!

Unscramble the letters to form the word that completes the sentence.

1. Until the boycott, African-Americans in Alabama had to sit at
   the _____ of the bus.   AKBC

2. Rosa Parks became one of the most important leaders of the
   _____ Rights movement.   LIIVC

3. African-Americans were also banned from eating at some
   _____ , and from many other places.   TAREURANTSS

Frederick Douglass

Frederick Douglass was a leader in the abolitionist movement, which fought to end slavery within the United States in the time leading up to the Civil War. Douglass was born a slave, but he escaped to the North, where slavery did not exist. He helped create an anti-slavery newspaper called The North Star.

Word scramble!

Unscramble the letters to form the word that completes the sentence.

1. Douglass sometimes gave President _____ advice. LILNONC

2. He wanted to give African-Americans the right to _____ . TVEO

3. Douglass was ambassador to the nation of _____ . IAHIT

Answers 1 LINCOLN   2 VOTE   3 HAITI

Booker T. Washington

Booker T. Washington was born into slavery on April 5, 1856. After the emancipation of the slaves, Washington was forced to get a job at age 9 to help support his poor family. In 1881, Washington became the Principal of Tuskegee Institute, a college for African-Americans in Tuskegee, Alabama. The school is still around today and is now called Tuskegee University. Washington wanted a good education for all African-Americans, and he worked his whole life to achieve this goal.

Word scramble!

Unscramble the letters to form the word that completes the sentence.

1. Booker T. Washington wrote a famous book about his life growing up, called "Up From _____".   LAVSRYE

2. Though she herself could not read or write, Washington's _____ bought him textbooks so he could learn.   ERMTHO

3. As a slave, Washington worked on a _____ , the type of farm on which most slaves were forced to work.   NLANPIOTAT

Jesse Owens

Olympic Gold Medal-winning track and field athlete

James Cleveland Owens was born in Oakville, Alabama in 1913 He was nine years old when his family moved to Cleveland, Ohio, where he received the nickname Jesse. When his new teacher asked his name, he replied that it was "J.C.," as he was called at the time. Because of his Southern accent, the teacher misheard the name as "Jesse," and the nickname stuck.

As a boy, Owens took what odd jobs he could find, working while training on the track and field team in junior high school. Owens' coach allowed him to practice before school so he could keep his after-school job at a shoe repair shop. After high school, he went on to compete for Ohio State University's track team. He set three world records and tied a fourth. Still, he was forced to live off campus with other African-American athletes, and when the team traveled, he stayed in "black-only" hotels. Despite those circumstances, he persisted in his training and competition and went on to win four gold medals in the 1936 Olympic Games in Germany.

Word scramble!

Unscramble the letters to form the word that completes the sentence.

1. The 1936 Summer Olympics took place in the German capital city of
   _____ .   NERBIL

2. Adi Dassler, the founder of athletic shoe company Adidas, persuaded Owens to wear Adidas shoes in the Olympic Games. This was the first known _____ of an African-American athlete.   HIPSPOORSNS

3. Owens' family moved from their home in Ohio during the Great _____ , when many African-Americans moved away from the South.   IOIGRANMT

Answers: 1. BERLIN   2. SPONSORSHIP   3. MIGRATION

W.E.B. Du Bois

Activist, journalist, sociologist

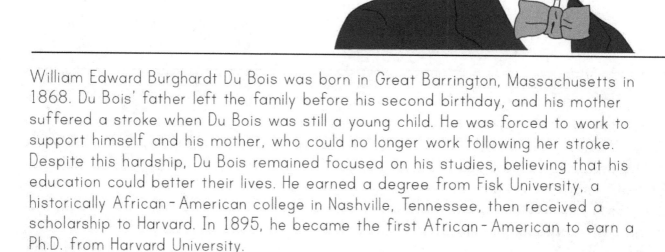

William Edward Burghardt Du Bois was born in Great Barrington, Massachusetts in 1868. Du Bois' father left the family before his second birthday, and his mother suffered a stroke when Du Bois was still a young child. He was forced to work to support himself and his mother, who could no longer work following her stroke. Despite this hardship, Du Bois remained focused on his studies, believing that his education could better their lives. He earned a degree from Fisk University, a historically African-American college in Nashville, Tennessee, then received a scholarship to Harvard. In 1895, he became the first African-American to earn a Ph.D. from Harvard University.

    He taught at the university level for several years, then went to work at Atlanta University, now called Clark Atlanta University, in Atlanta, Georgia. He created the university's department of social work, which exists today as the Whitney M. Young, Jr. School of Social Work. He became founder and editor of the NAACP's journal, The Crisis, which published African-American writers, including some who wrote during the Harlem Renaissance. He argued against Booker T. Washington's belief that African-Americans should accept segregation and the idea that they could be "separate but equal."

Word scramble!

Unscramble the letters to form the word that completes the sentence.

1. Du Bois worked to disprove the theory that African-Americans were biologically inferior to white Americans, called _____ racism. ICCIENSFTI

2. Du Bois was one of the founders of the NAACP, the National Association for the _____ of Colored People. NTDVAEAEMNC

3. In 1950, Du Bois ran for U.S. _____ from New York as a member of the American Labor Party. EOSRNAT

Martin Luther King, Jr.

Civil Rights leader

Martin Luther King, Jr. was born in Atlanta, Georgia in 1929. The son of a Baptist minister, he became one himself after studying at a theological seminary in Pennsylvania. There, he learned about the non-violent methods used by Mohandas Gandhi in protest of British colonization in India. King believed that African-Americans could gain their civil rights through peaceful demonstration and protest. He believed in methods such as the boycott, refusing to buy products or services from companies or people who discriminated against African-Americans.

In 1963, a civil rights march on Washington, D.C., called the March on Washington for Jobs and Freedom, helped make King internationally known. It was on the occasion of this march that King made his famous 'I Have A Dream' speech. He won the Nobel Peace Prize in 1964. That same year, the Civil Rights Act was passed, banning many types of discrimination against African-Americans.

Word scramble!

Unscramble the letters to form the word that completes the sentence.

1. His life as an activist began with the _____ Bus Boycott, started by Rosa Parks in the city it is named for.   NTRMOYGEOM

2. Martin Luther King, Jr. was _____ on April 4, 1968 in Memphis, Tennessee.   DANAITASSSES

3. In 1983, a _____ holiday was declared in honor of Martin Luther King, Jr. We still observe that holiday every January.   RALFEDE

George Washington Carver

Scientist, botanist and inventor

George Washington Carver was born into slavery some time between 1861 and 1864. No record exists to confirm the date of his birth. After the abolition of slavery, Carver's former masters, Moses and Susan Carver, raised George and his brother James as their own sons, teaching them reading and writing and encouraging George's intellectual pursuits. George took his new parents' last name.

A teacher at Simpson College in Iowa, where Carver was enrolled, noticed his talent for drawing flowers and encouraged him to study botany. Carver then went to study at Iowa State Agricultural College, where, to distinguish himself from another student named George Carver, he added Washington to his name. After a master's degree at Agricultural College, Booker T. Washington invited Carver to lead the agricultural department at the famed Tuskegee Institute. He remained there for 47 years, teaching former slaves farming techniques so they could support themselves.

Carver taught his students and agricultural professionals that crop rotation, the practice of planting different crops in the same fields year to year, could help soil retain its nutrients. He created many non-food products, everything from shaving cream to shoe polish to shampoo, from plants such as peanuts, sweet potatoes and pecans.

Word scramble!

Unscramble the letters to form the word that completes the sentence.

1. Though he is often falsely credited with having invented _____ _____, Carver did create more than 300 products using peanuts. UTAPEN RUTBET

2. Carver's birthplace was declared a national _____ , the first ever dedicated to an African-American. NTMEONUM

3. Many leaders consulted with Carver over agricultural matters, from Presidents of the United States to the Crown Prince of the country of _____ . ESENWD

Lewis and Clark

On May 14, 1804, Meriwether Lewis, William Clark and a team of 31 others set out on an expedition from St. Louis, Missouri. Their goal was to explore the lands and rivers of the western United States. At that time, the United States had no maps of that land or its rivers. President Thomas Jefferson hoped to find a Northwest Passage, a route of rivers that ships could use to cross from east to west. The team finally reached the Pacific Ocean in November of 1805, completing their expedition.

Word scramble!

Unscramble the letters to form the word that completes the sentence.

1. Another goal of the expedition was to make friends and set up trade with _____ American tribes .   TNAEIV

2. _____ , a Native American woman who knew the territory, helped guide the expedition.   AWAGEASAC

3. Along the way, Lewis and Clark saw many kinds of plants and _____ they had never seen before.   ALSMANI

Benjamin Franklin

Benjamin Franklin was a man of many talents. A scientist, author printer and inventor, he wrote a famous book called <u>Poor Richard's Almanac</u>, which is still being published today. An almanac is a book of important facts, such as weather reports, recipes and advice, printed yearly. He was the inventor of many things we still use today, like the lightning rod, bifocal glasses, a heater called the Franklin stove, and even swim fins!

Word scramble!

Unscramble the letters to form the word that completes the sentence.

1. Using a metal key tied to a kite, Franklin proved that lightning conducts _____ .   ITYLECECTRI

2. Franklin is responsible for the famous saying, "A penny saved is a penny _____ ".   NEDEAR

3. Franklin believed all people should be free, and spoke out against the practice of _____ .   YLASRVE

Answers: 1. ELECTRICITY   2. EARNED   3. SLAVERY

Thomas Edison

Thomas Edison was a scientist and inventor born in 1847. He is best known for his work with electric power. He invented a way to send power into homes and factories, and built a power station that created the electricity he sold. Edison helped design a type of light bulb similar to the one we use today, and he made many other discoveries in the field of electricity. He even invented a battery that could be used to power an electric car!

Word scramble!

Unscramble the letters to form the word that completes the sentence.

1. Edison created one of the first electric _____ , or power companies.

   TIIESULIT

2. He had over 1,000 _____ , which give rights and credit for inventions to their creator.

   PNTSATE

3. Edison also invented new ways of filming a _____ _____ , also known as a movie.

   TIOMNO UPREICT

Be a Text Detective 2nd GRADE

BE A DETECTIVE

When?

Where?

Who?

Why?

How?

What happened first?

_____ One day, other birds from the tree across the street made fun of the way she flapped her wings, so Jelly stopped flying.

_____ Jelly was flying high and having so much fun with her brothers and sisters that she forgot about the other birds. She learned that you enjoy the things you love more when you stop worrying about what others think.

_____ After a few days, Jelly was bored of walking everywhere and did not want to miss out on the fun.

Table of Contents

Be a Text Detective

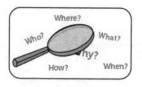

Questions First By Julie Williams

Is your child full of questions? Most kids are! With this activity, your child can ask away and develop some important reading and comprehension skills while he's at it.

A vital goal for young readers is the ability not just to decode text but to make real sense of it. Can your child keep all those characters straight and follow what's happening?

Here's an activity that teachers use all the time, and it works at home, too! It's simple and easy to set up, but it can lead to some very deep and complicated thinking, helping to develop those comprehension skills.

What You Need:

- Pad of sticky notes
- Pen
- Story book you plan to read to your child

What You Do:

1. Find a book you think is terrific and can't wait to read to your child. Read it front to back, just by yourself...no kid yet! What do you like about it? What does it teach?

2. Now go back, looking at each "spread" (the two pages you see when you hold the book open).

Ask yourself a question:
What's the most important thing happening in these two pages?

This will vary, of course. It may be a change in the action; it may be a new character; it may be the way a main character is feeling.

3. For at least five spreads, jot down an open-ended* question that you can ask your child to get at this main idea. Put your note on that page. For a chapter book you can do the same thing, selecting key spots in the book. For instance, on the page where a new character is introduced or a change in the story happens you could mark it.

* For example, you're reading "Curious George." You'll want to avoid close-ended questions such as "What color is George's fur?" This can feel too simple to your child, and too much like a quiz. Instead, ask questions about George himself: "How does George feel about his broken bicycle?" and especially focus on predictions: "Do you think he can get it fixed?"

4. Now read the book with your child, and savor it together. Each time you get to a posted question, stop to talk it over.

5. As you approach the end of the story, you will have had a rich conversation. Now bring it to a close by holding the book shut for the very last page or two.

Ask: OK, after all this, what do you think will happen? Join your child in making predictions, and then read together. How do you feel at the end? Did the author surprise you? What do you think?

6. Note: if you're making a "star chart" this is a great time to stick your evaluation on the wall! Moving forward, encourage your child to try writing some of his own sticky notes sometime on a familiar, favorite book and then reading the book to a younger child. **Nothing improves learning like teaching does.**

Even if your child is up to reading chapter books doing this exercise with a picture book can illustrate the point of asking questions. For picture books with significant text on the page a few stories you can try are *Twelve Dancing Princesses*, *Pegasus*, and *The Seven Voyages of Sinbad the Sailor*. **For** chapter books, you can also do the above steps at the chapter-level instead of individual spreads.

Example

SEQUENCE OF EVENTS

Read the story below, then number the illustrations in the order in which they took place in the story.

Lila's New Glasses

Lila was a girl who had trouble seeing. She loved to ride her bike, but she couldn't see well enough to know which way to turn. She loved to play soccer, but she could never see when the ball was coming her way! Most of all, Lila loved to go to school... but she always had a very hard time reading the lesson on the blackboard.

One day Lila's mother took her to the eye doctor. The eye doctor looked at Lila's eyes and instantly knew that Lila was going to need a pair of glasses. At first, Lila was very sad that she was going to have to wear glasses. The doctor told her that glasses help people see, and that once she had a pair of her own, she would be able to do all of the things that she loved! Lila decided that maybe it wouldn't be so bad after all.

Once Lila put on her glasses, she could not believe all the amazing things there were to see! She could ride her bike up and down the neighborhood. She could play soccer with her friends... and most exciting of all, Lila could finally read the lesson on the blackboard at school. Lila was so happy to finally be able to see, and wore her pair of glasses every single day.

ORGANIZE THE STORY

Oh no, the story has been all jumbled up. It's up to you to cut out the images and make the story make sense again.

Bonus Activity: Color in the images with your favorite colors.

Flying Jelly

These sentences are out of order and the story doesn't make sense!
Number the sentences below to put them in the correct order.

_____ One day, other birds from the tree across the street made fun of the way she flapped her wings, so Jelly stopped flying.

_____ Jelly was flying high and having so much fun with her brothers and sisters that she forgot about the other birds. She learned that you enjoy the things you love more when you stop worrying about what others think.

_____ After a few days, Jelly was bored of walking everywhere and did not want to miss out on the fun.

_____ A little red bird named Jelly loved to go flying with her brothers and sisters, but Jelly didn't flap her wings like everyone else.

_____ Despite being embarrassed she started flying again and ignored the older birds who teased her: "Yay! Jelly is flying!" cheered her siblings. "Wow! She can fly higher than older birds can."

_____ "There is nothing wrong with the way you flap your wings!" Her brothers and sisters begged her to fly with them.

Peanut and Kiki

These sentences are out of order and the story doesn't make sense!
Number the sentences below to put them in the correct order.

 _____ While sharing some cherries with Kiki, Peanut thought it would be fun to start a race. "Whoever can get around the lake twice and collect the most cherries wins all of the cherries."

 _____ As Peanut flew and Kiki swung around from tree to tree, they tore off branches with cherries on them.

 _____ While eating the cherries, she heard Peanut's stomach rumble. Kiki felt bad that she was not sharing her cherries with Peanut. "You can have some of these cherries if you are hungry," said Kiki. "Really? Thanks, Kiki," said Peanut.

 _____ A bird named Peanut was good friends with a monkey named Kiki. They spent a lot of time together sharing fruit and searching for bugs.

 _____ When they both made it around the lake twice, they stopped to count how many cherries they had collected. "Yay! I get all of the cherries!" yelled Kiki as she grabbed all of the cherries.

 _____"That's a great idea!" said Kiki. "Ready, set, go!" she said, and they both took off.

Rocky Sings at Sunrise

These sentences are out of order and the story doesn't make sense!
Number the sentences below to put them in the correct order.

_____ "I guess I don't sing as well as I thought," said Rocky to himself. The one camper who enjoyed Rocky's singing heard Rocky and said, "I love the way you sing, little bird. I'm sure the other campers do too, but you and the woodpecker are a little too loud."

_____ A sweet little bird named Rocky loved to sing loudly from his home in a Redwood tree. He woke up with the sunrise to sing along to the beat of woodpecker's pecking.

_____ One of the campers was awake and enjoying Rocky's singing, but the other campers were unhappy. "Why are those birds making so much noise?" groaned a grumpy camper.

_____ Rocky and the woodpecker made beautiful and soft music. The campers woke up one by one, and Rocky was excited to make them happy.

_____ One summer, some people came and camped under his tree. Rocky thought he would welcome them by singing for them early the next morning.

_____ The next morning, Rocky sang softly and the woodpecker pecked softly as well.

Find The Main Idea

The **_main idea_** is the most important idea in a paragraph. Sometimes, the main idea is the first sentence. Sometimes the main idea is in the middle or at the end. Read the paragraphs carefully. Circle the main idea.

Kittens need special care. You have to feed kittens twice a day. They have a lot of energy. You need to play with them often. Kittens will chew on almost anything they find. You have to watch them closely.

What is the main idea?

1. Kittens will chew on almost anything.

2. Kittens need special care.

The puppy began to eat, but then he stopped. He yawned and stretched. He chased his tail. He rolled over and barked. He licked his paw. Finally, he went back to his dish and finished eating.

What is the main idea?

1. The puppy likes to eat.

2. The puppy takes a long time to eat.

What's in a Story?

Read the story, then write the main idea in the middle box. Write one detail in each of the other boxes.

It's the first day of school! Ellie is very excited. She takes her new backpack and lunchbox to school. She is happy to see her friends in the classroom. The students like their teacher. Everyone has a good first day of school.

Detail:

Detail:

Main idea:

Detail:

Detail:

Story Order :Case 1

Read the story, then write the main idea in the top box.
Next, summarize three details and a conclusion in the remaining boxes.

The entire class decided that the movie they watched was very exciting. First, a princess was kidnapped from her castle. Next, the main character magically became a knight in shining armor. Finally, the knight crossed the forest and saved the princess. Clearly, the movie was full of adventure.

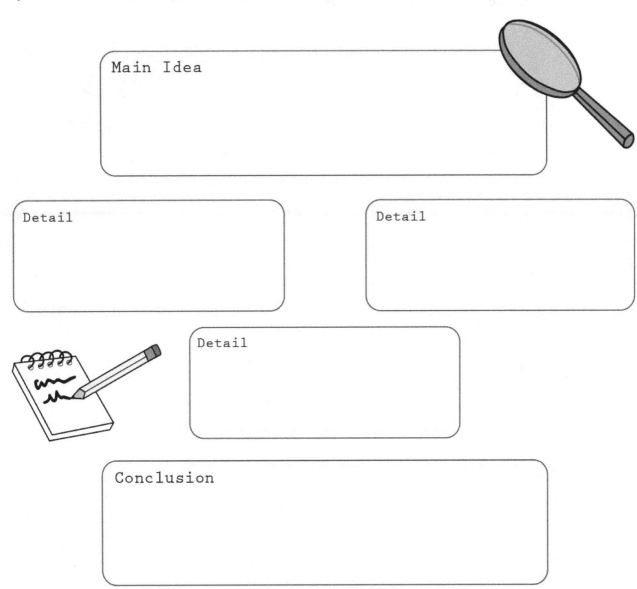

Main Idea

Detail

Detail

Detail

Conclusion

Story Order :Case 2

Read the story, then write the main idea in the top box.
Next, summarize three details and a conclusion in the remaining boxes.

The Smith family would remember this vacation for a long time. They liked going camping, and first they got ready months ahead by going on hikes regularly. On their vacation they hiked down to the bottom of the Grand Canyon. Then they rafted down part of the Colorado River which runs through the canyon. Their river guide was knowledgeable and friendly. And, everyone had a good sense of humor. All these things came together to make for a memorable trip.

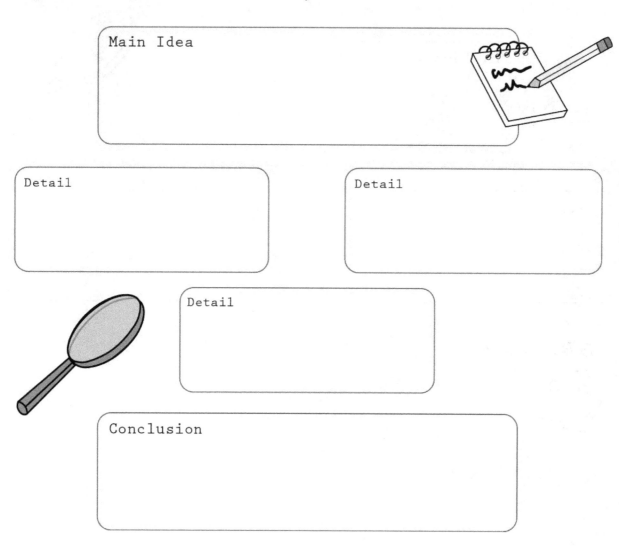

Main Idea

Detail

Detail

Detail

Conclusion

Cause and Effect

A cause is why something happens. An effect is what happens.

Example: Anna skipped breakfast, so she was hungry all morning.

cause   effect

Circle the best effect for each cause.

1. Jim did not study...
      so he made an A+ on the test.
      so he did poorly on the test.

2. The soccer team practiced everyday...
      and won the game.
      and lost the game.

3. There was a blizzard outside...
      so everyone went outside to play.
      so school was cancelled.

4. Ava felt sick...
      so Mom took her to the doctor.
      so I gave her some ice cream.

5. The girl tripped...
      and checked her messages.
      and skinned her knees.

6. I ate too much candy...
      and got a stomach ache.
      and felt great.

7. The team won...
      and the coach was sad.
      and they celebrated with a party.

8. The baby cried...
      so Dad held her.
      and she made Dad cry.

9. Tony took good care of his dog...
      and his dog was very happy.
      and his dog ran away.

10. Mary's hands were dirty after painting...
      so she washed them with soap and water.
      so she sat down to eat dinner.

Cause and Effect (1)

With Caroline the Carrot

Hi! I am Caroline the Carrot. Let's learn the difference between a *cause* and an *effect* together. A *cause* is the reason why something happens. An *effect* is what happens. Here is an example:

Because Bobby watered the garden daily,
            (cause)
the vegetables grew beautifully.
            (effect)

Circle the best way to end the sentence.

1. Jack is worried

    because he lost his homework.   because he got a present.

2. Because the sun came out,

    Andrew went to sleep.   Andrew went out to play.

3. Our teacher is happy

    because we did well on our tests.   because it is Tuesday.

4. Because Jim is nice,

    he likes the color blue.   he has a lot of friends.

5. Kristen's team won the match

    because she had fun.   because she scored a goal.

6. Because it is cold,

    Isabelle wore a jacket.   Isabelle learned to read.

7. My sister is sad

    because she lost her wallet.   because she ate dinner.

8. Because I did my chores,

    I woke up early.   I received my allowance.

Cause and Effect (2)

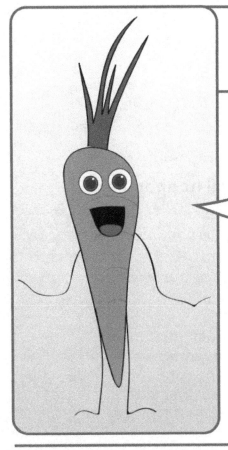

Let's learn some more about cause and effect. Read the stories below and underline the sentence that tells why something happened.

1. Mya was playing frisbee outside with her sister. Her sister threw the frisbee as hard as she could. It sailed over the neighbor's fence. Mya rang the neighbor's doorbell.

Why did Mya ring the doorbell?

She had a delivery for the neighbors.   She wanted to retrieve the frisbee.

She was going to the neighbor's house for lunch.

---

2. A hawk was soaring high above the trees. He soon spotted a rabbit darting through the forest. His stomach began to rumble. The hawk swooped down toward his prey.

Why did the hawk swoop down?

He likes exploring the forest.   He was hungry.   He saw his friend.

---

3. Danny was nervous to audition for the play. He tried his best to sing every note on key. When his audition was over, he was worried he wouldn't get the part he wanted. Danny was so happy when he saw the cast list.

Why was Danny happy?

He likes singing.   The audition was over.   He got the part he wanted.

---

4. Nancy and her friend Debbie decided to go out to dinner. Debbie forgot to close the window before they left. They enjoyed a delicious meal. When they got back to Nancy's house it was very cold.

Why was Nancy's house so cold?

Debbie forgot to close the window.   She went out to dinner with Debbie.

Nancy forgot to close the window.

The Man, the Boy, and the Donkey

Mission:
Read the story below. Can you predict what will happen next?

Once, a man and his son were going to the market with their donkey. As they walked a man passed them and said, "How silly. You are walking that donkey when you could be riding it instead. What is a donkey for but to ride on?"

Hearing this, the man put his boy on the donkey's back and they went on their way. But soon they passed a group of women, one of whom said: "You should be ashamed of yourself young man. Your father who is older than you should be riding and you should be walking." Red-faced and embarrassed the boy jumped down to have his father get up on the donkey.

They hadn't gone far when they passed a man and woman, one of whom said to the other: "Doesn't he know they can both fit on that donkey? His boy doesn't have to walk this dusty road."

What do you think the father and son will do next? Why?

_____

_____

_____

_____

Well, the man didn't know what to do, but at last he took his son up and sat him down in front of him on the donkey. They reached the town and people began to jeer and point at them. "You're overloading that poor donkey—you and your son both sitting there. You both look strong! You'd be better off carrying the donkey yourselves."

They got off of the donkey and tried to think what to do. At last they cut down a pole and tied the donkey's feet to it. With it tied to the pole like this they raised the pole to their shoulders and carried the donkey towards the bridge that lead to the market. This was difficult to do.

The townspeople laughed and heckled them so much that the donkey was frightened by everything going on. Its feet slipped loose from the ropes and it fell. Once it got to its feet again it ran away kicking and bucking.

"That will teach you," said an old man who had followed them. "Try to please everyone and you will please no one."

What was the moral of the story?

_____

_____

_____

_____

The Boy Who Cried Wolf

Mission:
Read the story below. Can you predict what will happen next?

Once upon a time in a mountain village, there was a boy who watched over the village's sheep. Being alone up in the hills was very boring. One day the boy thought it would be funny to scare the villagers and scream, "Wolf, wolf!" The villagers grabbed whatever they could and ran up the hill to scare off the wolf.

When they reached the top, they realized there was no wolf. They had been tricked by the mischievous boy. He laughed and laughed while the villagers walked angrily back down the hill. On another day the boy again called, "Wolf! Wolf!" tricking the villagers. They warned him that the next time they would no longer believe him. The boy shrugged at the warning and laid down for a nap.

What do you think will happen next? Why?

_____

_____

_____

_____

Keep reading...

One lazy afternoon, the boy heard a terrible sound. Before he could even prepare himself, a wolf appeared and chased the village's sheep! The boy screamed, "Wolf, wolf!" but having lied so many times, the people of the village just ignored him. With no one to help him fend off the wolf, the sheep all ran away and the boy was left crying on the hill.

Wolf!
Wolf!

What was the moral of the story?

_____

_____

_____

_____

The Ant and the Grasshopper

Mission:
Read the story below. Can you predict what will happen next?

Once there was an ant and a grasshopper who lived in a field.

Every day, Ant got up early and walked far to gather seeds. She balanced one seed on her head at a time, walked it back to her home, and then went again to the field to gather more. She was very small, so the walk was very long. She worked the whole day, without ever stopping to rest.

As Ant worked, Grasshopper spent his days playing music, lazing in the sun. "Why do you work so hard, Ant?" he laughed. "Summer is here! Why waste the sunshine gathering seeds.

What do you think Ant will do?
What do you think Grasshopper will do? Why?

_____

_____

_____

_____

_____

 **Keep reading...**

Ant ignored Grasshopper's teasing and continued gathering, which only made Grasshopper laugh even more. "You are a silly little ant," he said.

Autumn came, and then winter. The days were short. Snow fell on the farmer's field, burying the plants and seeds that had been so easy to get.

Grasshopper had no food to eat. "What will I do? I am hungry," Grasshopper said to himself. Then, he remembered how many seeds Ant had stashed away during the summer.

Grasshopper hurried to Ant's home. He knocked on her door. "Ant," he said, "Give me some seeds?"

Ant looked at Grasshopper. "I worked hard all summer long, while you laughed at me," Ant said. "You should have worked in the summer instead of singing and dancing. Then you would have a full belly now."

What was the moral of the story?

_____

_____

_____

_____

The Ant and the Grasshopper

We need your help, gumshoe! The story cards are mixed up and don't make sense. Please solve this case by cutting the cards out and putting them back in the correct order.

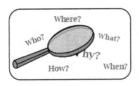

Make a Star Chart By Julie Williams

It's important for young readers to stop and reflect on what they have read and understood.

Here is a way to keep track of new books, mark the achievement of reading them, and most importantly, step back and think: Which ones were really, really great?

What You Need:

- 11" x 17" sheet of paper
- Markers
- Package of shiny gold stars
- 12" x 17" sheet of construction paper in a favorite color

What You Do:

1. Explain to your child that every week in the newspaper you can find ratings for all kinds of things. There are so many movies, for example, that we often rely on other people to help us narrow the choices based on their opinioins of what's good and bad and why. Sometimes that means we talk to friends; other times, we look in a newspaper, magazine, or TV to read the words of a critic. You might even want to look a review up together.

2. In this activity, invite your child to be a literary critic for the family. In this exciting new world of books, which ones are the very best? Which ones were just okay? Which ones were unbelievably bad? And most importantly in every case: Why?

3. Take your sheet of 11x17" paper and start by folding it vertically in thirds. Across the top, in block letters, help your child write a catchy title using her name, such as "Becca's Best Books." Your child may want to do the printing; it's also OK if you help.

4. Now take out those gold stars. Your left column is for the big winners—three gold stars! The middle column is for the books that were OK but not great—two stars. And the column on the right has no stars at all—that's for books your child decides are just plain awful.

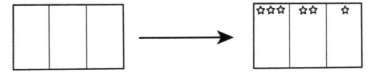

5. In clear writing below each category (parents, you may want to help with this), write your child's explanation of criteria. What makes a book really good? (This is obviously a conversation that will continue for a lifetime. Now's a great time to start! For young kids expect simple, concrete answers; that's just fine.

6. Mount your "star chart" on a construction paper frame, and invite your child to decorate it as she likes. Then tape it to a wall near a place where you and your child often read.

For the next several months, whenever you read together, stop and have a chat. How was that book? What column does it belong in? Write your "critic's choice" selections, and celebrate them. When the chart is full, write the dates it covers, and keep it. You and your child will have marked two marvelous accomplishments: a long list of books read...and the start of a lifelong conversation about what makes a book really great.

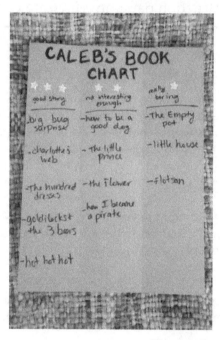

Example

Phonics Fun:
Vowels & Diphthongs

2nd GRADE

Table of Contents

Phonics Fun: Vowels and Diphthongs

Reading
SHORT VOWELS

a

Circle all objects below that have a short a sound. Then write the word under the picture.

e

Circle all objects below that have a short e sound. Then write the word under the picture.

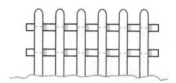

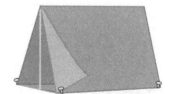

Circle all objects below that have a short i sound. Then write the word under the picture.

2nd Grade
Reading
SHORT VOWELS

O

Circle all objects below that have a short o sound. Then write the word under the picture.

2nd Grade
Reading
SHORT VOWELS
u

Circle all objects below that have a short u sound. Then write the word under the picture.

2nd Grade
Reading
LONG VOWELS
(a)

Circle all objects below that have a long **a** sound. Then write the word under the picture.

2nd Grade
Reading
LONG VOWELS

(e)

Circle all objects below that have a long e sound. Then write the word under the picture.

i

Circle all objects below that have a long i sound. Then write the word under the picture.

Reading
LONG VOWELS

(O)

Circle all objects below that have a long o sound. Then write the word under the picture.

Circle all objects below that have a long a sound. Then write the word under the picture.

Just Add E

Add an e to the end of these short vowel words to make new long vowel words.

tub → tub___

can → can___

pin → pin___

rob → rob___

cub → cub___

kit → kit___

tap → tap___

man → man___

Words Ending in Y

All of the words in the word box end in **y**.
If the y word has a **long e** sound, like **baby**,
write the word under the baby.
If the y word has a **long i** sound, like **spy**,
write the word under the spy.

bunny	very	my	sky	happy
fly	cry	shiny	penny	shy

baby

spy

_____

_____

_____

_____

_____

_____

_____

_____

AUTO Diphthongs

A diphthong is a pair of vowels that make a sound.
"AU" makes the sound in "AUTO."

Finish the sentences with one of the words below.

sauce   taught   autumn   fault

_____ always arrives before winter.

We were _____ the ABC's in kindergarten.

I like tomato _____ on my spaghetti.

It wasn't my _____ that the glass broke.

Find and circle the words with the AU sound.

Because
Caught
Audio
Daughter
Faucet
Vault
Auction
Taut

```
C U I D F I E A F E C V
E D T U T G C U A A T R
C G U L A T T U U A G A
C A C I R N T T C U C U
G I O A T A U O E C C D
A E A T A C A U T T A I
T A U T T U T S E I U O
D A U G H T E R U O G E
U C A H B A D T U N H C
V A U L T H L G B T T I
B E C A U S E A A T H A
T T A N D T G I C U I S
```

The words could
be horizontal
or vertical.

ANSWER

(answer grid shown inverted)

BOIL Diphthongs

A diphthong is a pair of vowels that make a sound.
"OI" makes the sound in "BOIL."

Finish the sentences with one of the words below.

join   spoil   soil   voice

The scary witch had a screechy _____ .

I planted the watermelon seeds in the _____ .

I would like to _____ the Boy Scouts.

If you leave the milk out, it will _____ .

Find and circle the words with the OI sound.

Coin

Oil

Point

Coil

Choice

Toil

Rejoice

Foil

```
R E J O I C E O I L O I
T I L O I I O C I I C L
I R T O O C O I L O H I
I I F O I L L I C F O R
I L O T L I C O O C I H
T L L I O P H O P O C N
O I E E J T R I I I E I
N J L P T L C C P I O F
T N J P L O T T O O E E
I E E C C C I O I I N P
T O I L L I P N N I C O
C O I N O C O I T O O C
```

The words could
be horizontal
or vertical.

ANSWER

```
C O I N O C O I T O O C
T O I L L I P N N I C O
I E E C C C I O I I N P
T N J P L O T T O O E E
N J L P T L C C P I O F
O I E E J T R I I I E I
T L L I O P H O P O C N
I L O T L I C O O C I H
I I F O I L L I C F O R
I R T O O C O I L O H I
T I L O I I O C I I C L
R E J O I C E O I L O I
```

CLOUD Diphthongs

A diphthong is a pair of vowels that make a sound.
"OU" makes the sound in "CLOUD."

Finish the sentences with one of the words below.

pound   loud   mountain   mouth

The dentist said, "Open your _____ ."

We got our new dog from the _____ .

I love to hike on the _____ .

Turn down the music! It's too _____ .

Find and circle the words with the OU sound.

About
Out
Sound
Our
Around
House
Found
South

```
U S D A O D S D A S N N
O U U B N U F H U N E D
O D O D A E U H O U S E
U H B O S O S D U U T H
U U T T H A A B O U T F
S D U O S O U T H N U O
O T O U U O T O F N F U
H A O T O O O R H U N N
A R O U N D O U T S E D
S T N H U O U T U H A D
O U U O H U O D D A B O
O U R F O T S O U N D D
```

The words could
be horizontal
or vertical.

ANSWER

```
U S D A O D S D A S N N
O U U B N U F H U N E D
O D O D A E U H O U S E
U H B O S O S D U U T H
U U T T H A A B O U T F
S D U O S O U T H N U O
O T O U U O T O F N F U
H A O T O O O R H U N N
A R O U N D O U T S E D
S T N H U O U T U H A D
O U U O H U O D D A B O
O U R F O T S O U N D D
```

1̶2̶3̶ COUNT Diphthongs

A diphthong is a pair of vowels that make a sound.
"OU" can make the sound in "COUNT."

Finish the sentences with one of the words below.

blouse   ground   bouncy   shout

My mom said, "Don't _____. I can hear you."

For my birthday, I got a red _____ ball.

I spilled juice all over my new _____.

During recess, I tripped and fell to the _____.

Find and circle the words with the OU sound.

Round
Foul
Nouns
Thousand
Sour
Outside
Abound
Couch

```
O O E O O O E E A S F S
O D O N O O F N I H O L
O O A H O H N U T D U S
D O H A U U N C H R L S
U D O O A U O O O O A S
U O N S U R U U U U F N
U I O A U L N C S N O R
H E H H O O S H A D E A
O U T S I D E U N U O N
D U U T N O U C D H N R
U S O U R S S O U R T E
C E U A B O U N D O N N
```

The words could
be horizontal
or vertical.

ANSWER

```
N N O D N U O B A U E C
U S O U R S S O U R T E
D U U T N O U C D H N R
N O N U E D I S T U O
A E D A H S O O H H E H
R O N S C N L U A O I U
N F U U U U R U S N O U
S A O O O U A O O D U
S L R H C N U U A H O D
S U D T U N H O H A O O
L O H I N F O O N O D O
S F S A E O O O E O O
```

SAW Diphthongs

A diphthong is a pair of vowels that make a sound.
"AW" makes the sound in "SAW."

Finish the sentences with one of the words below.

lawn   yawn   hawk   crawl

The baby just learned to _____ .

We watched a _____ circle in the sky.

To get allowance, I have to mow the _____ .

During math class, I try not to _____ .

Find and circle the words with the AW sound.

Draw
Straw
Dawn
Slaw
Pawn
Law
Claw
Fawn

```
W A W W L W F F R A A S
A N D R A W C A L S W W
W R L W L L W A W L W A
S A W L N C W N C A C A
A D A T F D W N A W A P
W W F W A A A P W W A A
A N P A W N L W W R N R
A W A N W L A W A A W P
P P W D P F A W N A R N
C L A W W N R A D A W N
A S A A R A C F N N A W
W F W S T R A W W A W A
```

The words could
be horizontal
or vertical.

ANSWER

```
W A W W L W F F R A A S
A N D R A W C A L S W W
W R L W L L W A W L W A
S A W L N C W N C A C A
A D A T F D W N A W A P
W W F W A A A P W W A A
A N P A W N L W W R N R
A W A N W L A W A A W P
P P W D P F A W N A R N
C L A W W N R A D A W N
A S A A R A C F N N A W
W F W S T R A W W A W A
```

JEWEL Diphthongs

A diphthong is a pair of vowels that make a sound.
"EW" makes the sound in "JEWEL."

Finish the sentences with one of the words below.

knew   flew   blew   dew

The wind _____ hard during the storm.

Vampire bats _____ during the dark night.

I studied for the test, so I _____ the answers.

In the morning, the grass was wet with _____.

Find and circle the words with the EW sound.

Brew
New
Chew
Drew
Grew
Stew
Renew
Threw

```
G H R H W R W E R T W T
R W W W N W B R R H E E
E E W E N R R D E R R S
W R W E E W E R E E E W
R N E E H N W E S W E S
E R E H G E R W N E E T
G N R W W C E D W C H E
T H T R E H N W R E W W
E E T T W E E W W W R W
E W G H E W E W W W E T N
R E N E W W N E W E N E
R G N W T N W R C S W H
```

The words could
be horizontal
or vertical.

ANSWER

```
R G N W T N W R C S W H
R E N E W W N E W E N E
E W G H E W E W W W E T N
E E T T W E E W W W R W
T H T R E H N W R E W W
G N R W W C E D W C H E
E R E H G E R W N E E T
R N E E H N W E S W E S
W R W E E W E R E E E W
E E W E N R R D E R R S
R W W W N W B R R H E E
G H R H W R W E R T W T
```

OWL Diphthongs

A diphthong is a pair of vowels that make a sound.
"OW" makes the sound in "OWL."

Finish the sentences with one of the words below.

cows   clown   meow   flowers

I like to pick _____ in the garden.

Our new little kitten said _____ !

A funny _____ performed at the circus.

Black and white _____ grazed in the field.

Find and circle the words with the OW sound.

Power
Drown
Wow
Town
Plow
Brown
Growl
Vowel

```
D R O W N O O V W G L O
G N N T O E V R L N R W
W P W W B N W W N N O B
L O R R W R O T O R V L
O O P N D W B O W T O W
R O O W N O R R E R W L
L E W W O P L O W W E E
N W O V W D O N O W L O
B R O W N G R O W L T W
O W O W W W T D L W O O
R W G P O W E R W D W N
R L W O W N G B T L N W
```

The words could
be horizontal
or vertical.

ANSWER

```
R L W O W N G B T L N W
R W G P O W E R W D W N
O W O W W W T D L W O O
B R O W N G R O W L T W
N W O V W D O N O W L O
L E W W O P L O W W E E
R O O W N O R R E R W L
O O P N D W B O W T O W
L O R R W R O T O R V L
W P W W B N W W N N O B
G N N T O E V R L N R W
D R O W N O O V W G L O
```

TOY Diphthongs

A diphthong is a pair of vowels that make a sound.
"OY" makes the sound in "TOY."

Finish the sentences with one of the words below.

joyful   royal   enjoy   loyal

The queen led the _____ parade.

Christmas is a _____ holiday!

I _____ sleeping in late on Saturday.

My dog is a _____ friend to me.

Find and circle the words with the OY sound.

Boy
Joy
Soy
Decoy
Cowboy
Toy
Ahoy
Annoy

```
D O B H Y O Y N N S Y W
E O A S B Y Y H D O O O
C N T H W B N Y O C Y Y
O N O A Y O O O T O A J
Y B A J C O W B O Y S B
T Y C O O Y O O Y Y O O
O A H O Y B O Y N O Y Y
Y O O E O S B C N O T B
Y O N Y J Y E O Y Y J N
C O N C Y O B A Y B A H
S A A N N O Y N C T B Y
J O Y Y B Y Y J Y C Y W
```

The words could
be horizontal
or vertical.

ANSWER

```
T O Y Y B A Y J Y C Y W
S A A N N O Y N C T B Y
C O N C Y O B A Y B A H
Y O N Y J Y E O Y Y J N
Y O O E O S B C N O T B
O A H O Y B O Y N O Y Y
T Y C O O Y O O Y Y O O
Y B A J C O W B O Y S B
O N O A Y O O O T O A J
C N T H W B N Y O C Y Y
E O A S B Y Y H D O O O
D O B H Y O Y N N S Y W
```

Oh Boy!

Write **oi, oy, ou,** or **ow** to complete the word.
Use the pictures as clues.

h _ _ se

b _ _

c _ _

c _ _ n

cl _ _ d

m _ _ se

cl _ _ n

_ _ l

s _ _ l

f _ _ l

t _ _

Stu-pen-dous
Syllables

Joshua

Syllable 1	Syllable 2	Syllable 3	How many?
Josh	u	a	3

January

JAN
31

1   2   3   4

saxophone

sax

caterpillar

cat | er | pil | lar

alligator

1 2 3 4

Table of Contents

Stu-pen-dous Syllables

Syllables

A syllable is a word or part of a word that is one beat long.
The word **but** has 1 syllable, **butter** has 2 syllables,
and **butterfly** has 3 syllables.

Read each word out loud, and count the syllables.
Write each word on the correct list.

tomorrow   syllable   cat   hamster   also   tonight   sing
done   mittens   monster   important   company

1	2	3
_____	_____	_____
_____	_____	tomorrow
_____	_____	_____
_____	_____	_____
_____	_____	_____

Fill in the chart by splitting the words into syllables.

	1	2	3
goldfish	gold	fish	_____
rainstorm	_____	_____	_____
spaceship	_____	_____	_____
classroom	_____	_____	_____
haircut	_____	_____	_____
newspaper	_____	_____	_____
skyscraper	_____	_____	_____

Syllables

A syllable is a word or part of a word that is one beat long.
Read each word out loud, while clapping for each syllable.
Circle the number of syllables for each word.

bones

1 2 3

elephant

1 2 3

net

1 2 3

flowers

1 2 3

baby

1 2 3

banana

1 2 3

Syllables

A syllable is a word or part of a word that is one beat long.
Read each word out loud, while clapping for each syllable.
Circle the number of syllables for each word.

duckling

(1) (2) 3 4

mouse

1 2 3 4

alligator

1 2 3 4

walrus

1 2 3 4

dinosaur

1 2 3 4

butterfly

1 2 3 4

Syllables

Color by syllables!

Read the words in the picture out loud and count the syllables.
Color the snake according to the color chart.

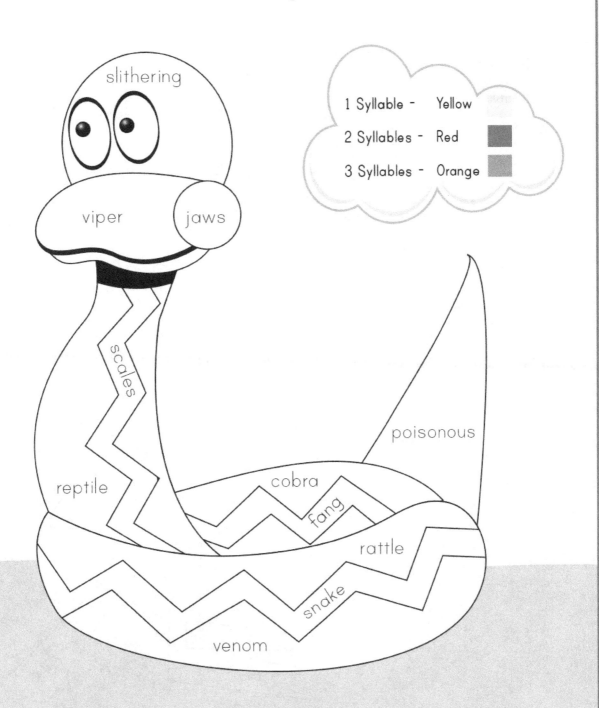

1 Syllable - Yellow

2 Syllables - Red

3 Syllables - Orange

slithering

viper   jaws

scales

reptile

poisonous

cobra

fang

rattle

snake

venom

Syllables

Color by syllables!

Read the words in the picture and count the syllables.
Color the bird according to the color chart.

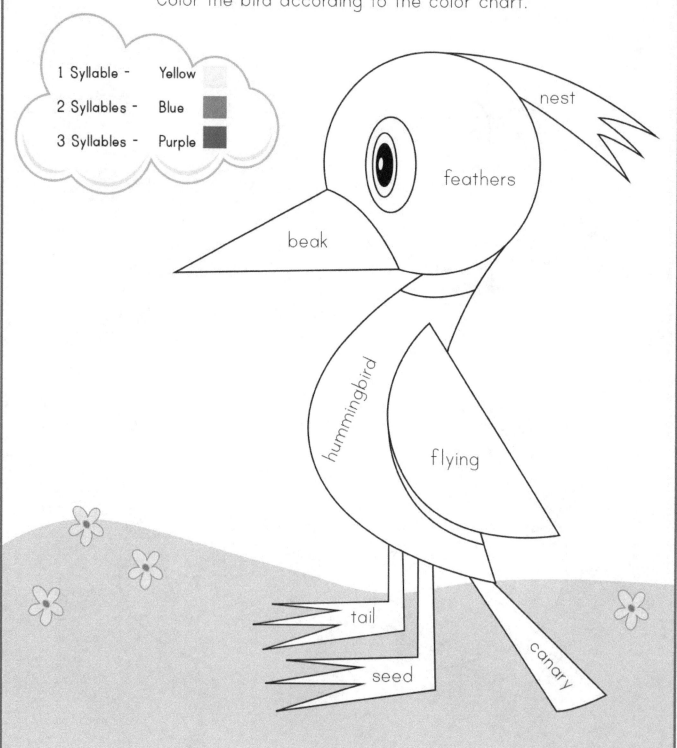

1 Syllable - Yellow

2 Syllables - Blue

3 Syllables - Purple

nest

feathers

beak

hummingbird

flying

tail

seed

canary

Syllables

With the VCV pattern (vowel, consonant, vowel),
a consonant between two vowels sticks with the second vowel.

Write down the number of syllables and draw a slash between the syllables.

HINT: Each syllable has one vowel sound. Divide the syllables BEFORE consonants.

__2__ fi/ner   _____ respect

_____ teacher   _____ trophy

_____ protect   _____ moment

_____ silent   _____ music

Read each three syllable word out loud. Finish dividing each word into syllables.

HINT: Divide the syllables BEFORE consonants

saxophone

negative

gravity

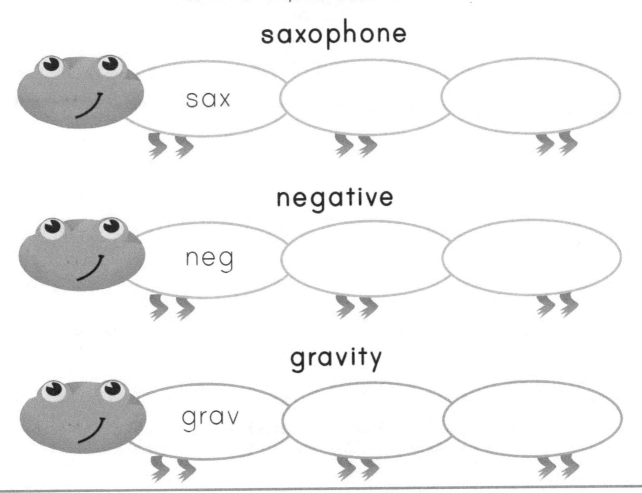

Syllables

With the VCV spelling pattern,
a consonant between two vowels sticks with the second vowel.

VCV   Not VCV

Cut out the name of each word. Read each word out loud.
Does the word follow the VCV rule? Paste each word in the correct column.

| chosen | giggle | girl | student |
| quarrel | between | costume | nature |

Syllables

Words that follow the VCCV pattern.

Think of VCCV words as a peanut butter and jelly sandwich. The peanut butter and jelly are the consonants, and bread are the vowels. So, when you split up the word into syllables, the consonants always stick to the vowels!

r a b / b i t

Read each word out loud, counting the syllables.
Write down the number of syllables and draw a slash between the syllables.
HINT: Each syllable has one vowel sound. Divide the syllables BETWEEN consonants.

___2___ fun/ny   _____ pillar

_____ mattress   _____ tissue

_____ pretty   _____ husband

_____ parrot   _____ certain

_____ mirror   _____ until

_____ giggle   _____ rescue

_____ happen   _____ chapter

_____ raccoon   _____ welcome

Syllables

With VCCV words, each syllable has one vowel sound.
Syllables are divided between consonants.

VCCV	Not VCCV

Cut out each word. Read each word out loud, counting the syllables.
Does it follow the VCCV rule? Paste each word in the correct column.

raccoon	insect	vulture	fox
lion	stork	monkey	shark

Syllables

VCV and VCCV Syllable Pattern Review

Count syllables then draw a slash
between the syllables.

VCV pattern (vowel, consonant, vowel).
Divide the syllables before consonants.

__2__ tro/phy	_____ teacher
_____ because	_____ student
_____ either	_____ chosen
_____ believe	_____ acre
_____ enough	_____ rider

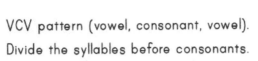

VCCV pattern (vowel, consonant, consonant vowel).
The consonants always stick to the vowels.

__2__ quar/rel	_____ essay
_____ raccoon	_____ announce
_____ cellar	_____ athlete
_____ gossip	_____ husband
_____ appeal	_____ costume
_____ mattress	_____ welcome
_____ terrace	_____ consume

Syllables

In "R-Controlled" syllable words, a vowel is followed by the letter "R".
HINT: The "R" gives the vowel a different sound.

R-Controlled

Not R-Controlled

Cut out the name of each word. Read each word out loud. Does the word follow the "R Controlled" rule? Paste each word in the correct column below.

turkey	run	baker	rabbit
pretty	shark	rough	bird

Syllables

A "Silent-E" syllable ends in an E, has one consonant before the E, and one vowel before the consonant. The pattern is: VCE.

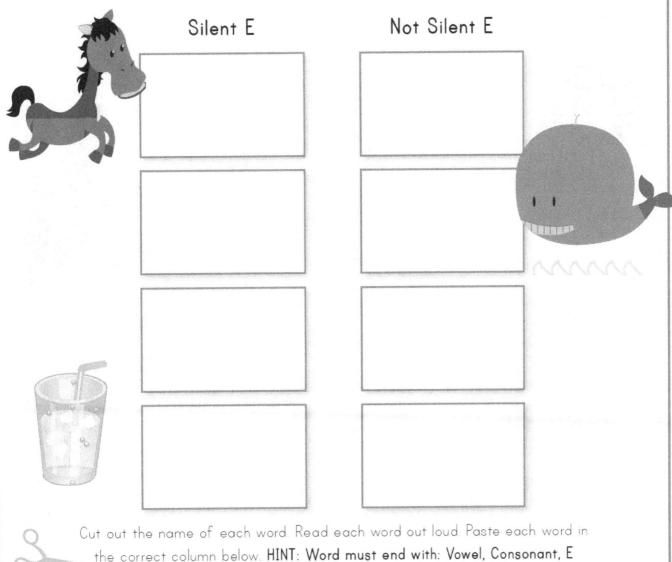

Silent E   Not Silent E

Cut out the name of each word. Read each word out loud. Paste each word in the correct column below. **HINT: Word must end with: Vowel, Consonant, E**

whale	little	ice	dye
able	tune	horse	hare

Syllables

With "Consonant-LE" syllables a consonant is followed by "LE".
The "LE" makes the last syllable.

Consonant LE

Not Consonant LE

Cut out the name of each word. Read each word out loud. Paste each word in the correct column below. **HINT: A consonant must be before the LE.**

| turtle | bubble | puzzle | peephole |
| kale | apple | parole | sale |

Syllables

Read each month, clapping for each syllable.
Circle the number clapping hands for each syllable.

	1	2	3	4
January	👏	👏	👏	👏
February	👏	👏	👏	👏
March	👏	👏	👏	👏
April	👏	👏	👏	👏
May	👏	👏	👏	👏
June	👏	👏	👏	👏
July	👏	👏	👏	👏
August	👏	👏	👏	👏
September	👏	👏	👏	👏
October	👏	👏	👏	👏
November	👏	👏	👏	👏
December	👏	👏	👏	👏

Syllables

Read the word out loud, and clap your hands for each syllable. Circle the number clapping hands for each syllable.

	1	2	3	4
baseball	👍	👍	👍	👍
catch	👍	👍	👍	👍
umpire	👍	👍	👍	👍
infielder	👍	👍	👍	👍
inning	👍	👍	👍	👍
championship	👍	👍	👍	👍
throw	👍	👍	👍	👍
doubleheader	👍	👍	👍	👍

Syllables

Syllables in Names

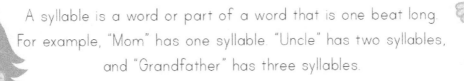

A syllable is a word or part of a word that is one beat long. For example, "Mom" has one syllable. "Uncle" has two syllables, and "Grandfather" has three syllables.

Practice counting syllables in names of people you know.

Write in the names of 5 people you know. Read each name out loud, clapping as you count each syllable.

Name	Syllable 1	Syllable 2	Syllable 3	How many?
Joshua	Josh	u	a	3

Write your first name here: _____

How many syllables are there? _____

Write your last name here: _____

How many syllables are there? _____

Syllables
Syllables in Animals

A syllable is a word or part of a word that is one beat long.
For example, "cat" has one syllable. "Monkey" has two syllables,
and "elephant" has three syllables.

Practice counting syllables in the names of different kinds of animals

Write in the names of 5 animals. Read each name out loud,
clapping as you count each syllable.

Name	Syllable 1	Syllable 2	Syllable 3	How many?
elephant	el	a	phant	3

Write the name of your pet (or a pet you know): _____

How many syllables are there? _____

Write the name of a cartoon animal: _____

How many syllables are there? _____

Syllables

Read long words!

Did you know you can read, write and understand longer words
if you break them down into syllables?

Write each syllable in a separate box. Then read the word out loud!

caterpillar	cat	er	pil	lar
difference				
snowmobile				
dishwasher				
emergency				
interesting				
porcupine				
thermometer				
bumblebee				
punctuation				
disappointed				
grandmother				

Syllables
In a Haiku

A haiku is a Japanese poem that is often about nature and the seasons.
Haikus always have three lines and a specific syllable count.
Read each Haiku, and write how many syllables are in each line.

Summer has faded ___5___

Leaves falling, gold and crimson _____

Autumn has begun _____

As the wind does blow _____

Across the trees, I see the _____

Buds blooming in May _____

Whiteness all around _____

Wind and cold and sun abound _____

Who would end this joy? _____

Now write your own haiku, and draw a picture to go with it!

1. _____

2. _____

3. _____

Syllables
In Limericks

A limerick is funny poem with five lines, and a set pattern of syllables.
Read the limericks below, then write how many syllables are in each line.
Try clapping each syllable to help you count.

He's a funny bird, the pelican _____9_____

His beak holds more than his belly can _____

He can hold in his beak _____

Enough food for a week _____

And I don't know how the heck he can! _____

There was an young boy of Peru _____

Who dreamt he was eating his shoe _____

He woke up in the night _____

With a terrible fright _____

And found it was perfectly true! _____

There was a young lady from Niger _____

Who smiled as she rode on a tiger _____

They returned from the ride _____

With the lady inside _____

A smile on the face of the tiger! _____

Humpback Anglerfish

It has a lantern that grows from the top of its head to attract prey.

It has long, sharp teeth for eating other creatures twice its own size.

It has tiny fins for swimming very slowly. because of its attractive lantern, it doesn't need to be fast to catch prey.

Table of Contents

Text Detective: Weird Animals

Fact or Opinion?
The Basking Shark and More

Read each sentence below and decide if it's a fact or an opinion.
Circle your answer.

1. The tube-nosed fruit bat helps new plants to grow by spreading seeds in its poop!   FACT   OPINION

2. The tube-nosed fruit bat's bugging eyes and pointy ears make it look like an alien.   FACT   OPINION

3. The Cthulhu Larvae travel in groups of 300 to 600 and eat mud.   FACT   OPINION

4. A nickname for the Cthulhu Larvae is sea pig.   FACT   OPINION

5. It would be terrifying to encounter a wolf fish.   FACT   OPINION

6. Sometimes, a wolf fish will jump out of the water and onto the shore to attack its prey.   FACT   OPINION

Fact or Opinion?
The Basking Shark and More

Read each sentence below and decide if it's a fact or an opinion.
Circle your answer.

7. The basking shark is the second-largest fish on the planet.

FACT   OPINION

8. The basking shark is harmless to humans and swims slowly with their mouths open to catch plankton, fish eggs, larvae, and other small sea creatures.

FACT   OPINION

9. Even though it looks scary, the star nosed mole is my favorite animal.

FACT   OPINION

10. This mole's sensitive nose can pick up tiny vibrations in the ground.

FACT   OPINION

Fact or Opinion?
The Blobfish and More

Read each sentence below and decide if it's a fact or an opinion.
Circle your answer.

1. The blobfish is made of a jelly-like substance and has almost no muscles.　　FACT　OPINION

2. It's awful that the blobfish is endangered because of harmful fishing trawlers.　　FACT　OPINION

3. If you see an aye-aye, that's a sign that something bad will happen to you.　　FACT　OPINION

4. The aye-aye is a superstitious symbol of death to the people of Madagascar.　　FACT　OPINION

5. The barking spider doesn't really bark, but its bite does cause several hours of vomiting.　　FACT　OPINION

6. The barking spider is a type of tarantula and typically catches insects in addition to lizards, frogs, and small birds.　　FACT　OPINION

Fact or Opinion?
The Blobfish and More

Read each sentence below and decide if it's a fact or an opinion.
Circle your answer.

7. The Cantor's giant soft-shelled turtle is able to extend its neck incredibly fast.   FACT   OPINION

8. People should make a big effort to help the endangered soft-shelled turtle survive.   FACT   OPINION

9. The flying snake sounds like a mythological creature.   FACT   OPINION

10. The flying snake is likely someone's worst nightmare.   FACT   OPINION

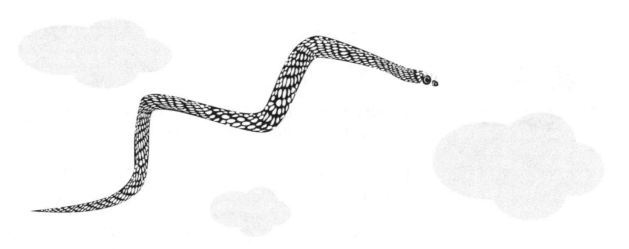

Fact or Opinion?
The Dumbo Octopus and More

Read each sentence below and decide if it's a fact or an opinion.
Circle your answer.

1. The Dumbo octopus is the cutest sea creature.   FACT   OPINION

2. The Dumbo octopus uses its ear-like flaps to help him swim around in the ocean.   FACT   OPINION

3. The Dumbo octopus hovers at the very bottom of the ocean, slightly above the seafloor.   FACT   OPINION

4. It would be so cool to touch a Dumbo octopus.   FACT   OPINION

5. The Superb bird of paradise uses its impressive feathers to court female birds.   FACT   OPINION

6. I would be scared of the male Superb bird of paradise.   FACT   OPINION

7. The Superb bird of paradise reminds me of a cartoon.   FACT   OPINION

8. The Superb bird of paradise also dances for the female bird to get her attention.   FACT   OPINION

Answers: 1. O; 2. F; 3. F; 4. O; 5. F; 6. O; 7. O; 8. F

Facts and Opinions:
Goliath Birdeat er

Janet went on vacation and saw something terrifying. She wrote about it in her journal. Underline sentences that are facts in black. Underline sentences that are opinions in orange.

I think South America has the scariest spiders ever! While hiking yesterday, I saw a huge spider that was black and furry. Mom told me that it's a Goliath birdeater, one of the largest spiders in the world. It is a type of tarantula and lives in the rainforests of South America. It got its name when a scientist saw it eating a hummingbird. I'm glad I didn't see it eating anything! It is harmless to humans, just like most other tarantulas. Their sting is only a little bit poisonous to humans. I'm relieved that Goliath birdeaters only live in South America. It'll be cool to tell all my friends back home about seeing this giant spider.

Write a sentence about your opinion of the Goliath birdeater.

_____

_____

_____

_____

Pictures Have a Lot to Say

The earth is full of strange animals. The aye-aye, for example, is a funny-looking creature. You can learn a lot about an animal just by looking at its picture.

Example: Aye-aye

Large ears to listen for echoes when tapping on tree trunks. (That helps it to find insect larvae.)

Very long middle finger to tap on tree trunks and pull out the insect larvae inside to eat.

Long, bushy tail for balance when climbing trees.

What about this odd-looking creature? Try to answer the questions below by studying its picture. Then, check out the answer sheet to learn more.

1. What type of creature is this: mammal, fish, reptile, or bird?

2. Does it live on land or in the sea?

3. Do you think it is a carnivore or herbivore?

Pictures Have a Lot to Say #2

What can you tell about an animal just by looking at the picture?

Example: Jack Rabbit

Big, pointy ears to hear very well.

Fur means that it's a mammal.

Small, slender body to easily hide in grassy areas.

Long hind legs to jump very high and run away from predators very fast.

Try to guess some things about this cute little creature. What can you tell about this animal just by looking at it?

1. What type of creature is this: mammal, fish, reptile, or bird?

_____

_____

2. Why do you think its ears are so large?

_____

_____

3. Why do you think it has such long legs and tail?

_____

_____

With and Without a Picture:
Narwhal

Narwhals are rare, medium-sized whales found in the Arctic Ocean. They eat shrimp, squid, and fish. Although they usually move slowly, they can be very fast when chased by predators. Their natural predators include polar bears and orcas (also called killer whales). They are capable of diving 5,000 feet beneath the surface of the ocean. They travel in groups of 10 to 20, called pods. They can communicate with each other using sounds like squeals and clicks. In summers, narwhals move closer to shore. In winters, they are farther out to sea and live under ice.

Show what you know. Write down three facts that you learned about narwhals.

1. _____

2. _____

3. _____

With and Without a Picture:
Narwhal (Part 2)

Narwhals are rare, medium-sized whales found in the Arctic Ocean. They eat shrimp, squid, and fish. Although they usually move slowly, they can be very fast when chased by predators. Their natural predators include polar bears and orcas (also called killer whales). They are capable of diving 5,000 feet beneath the surface of the ocean. They travel in groups of 10 to 20, called pods. They can communicate with each other using sounds like squeals and clicks. In summers, narwhals move closer to shore. In winters, they are farther out to sea and live under ice.

Write two things that you learned from the picture.

1. _____

....

==

....

==

....

2. _____

....

==

....

==

....

With and Without a Picture:
Narwhal (Part 3)

How does having a picture with the text change what you know about the animal?

_____

....

_____

....

_____

....

_____

The narwhal is called "the unicorn of the ocean" because of the large tusk on its face. The tusk is actually a tooth and can grow up to nine feet long! Only the male narwhals have this spiral tooth. Sometimes, they clash their tusks against each other. Scientists guess that they do this as a way to fight, communicate, or impress female narwhals. Scientists aren't really sure why they have this tooth!

Write your own opinion on why male narwhals have a long tusk.

_____

....

_____

....

_____

....

_____

....

_____

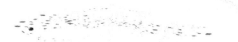

With and Without a Picture:
Olm

The olm is a blind salamander found in European caves. It lives underwater in complete darkness. Unlike other salamanders, it never leaves the water. Instead, it remains underwater at all times and swims like an eel. Because it can't see, it has an incredible sense of smell, taste, and touch. It can feel sound waves in the water and vibrations in the ground. It eats small crabs, snails, and insects. Food can be scarce in a cave, but the olm can eat large amounts of food at a time and then store all the nutrients for later. It can go for as long as 10 years without food! It can live for more than 58 years.

Show what you know. Write down three facts about the olm that you learned in this paragraph.

1.

2.

3.

With and Without a Picture:
Olm(Part 2)

The olm is a blind salamander found in European caves. It lives underwater in complete darkness. Unlike other salamanders, it never leaves the water. Instead, it remains underwater at all times and swims like an eel. Because it can't see, it has an incredible sense of smell, taste, and touch. It can feel sound waves in the water and vibrations in the ground. It eats small crabs, snails, and insects. Food can be scarce in a cave, but the olm can eat large amounts of food at a time and then store all the nutrients for later. It can go for as long as 10 years without food! It can live for more than 58 years.

Write two things that you
learned from the picture.

1.

2.

When you read about the olm, did you imagine it to look like it does in this picture?

Your Favorite Animal

Pick your favorite animal and learn more about it! With a grown-up, go online or to your local library to find some facts about your favorite animal.

Write your opinion:

The _____ is my favorite animal

because _____

Write 3 facts you learned about your favorite animal.

1. _____

2. _____

3. _____

Draw a picture of the animal that shows the 3 facts above.

Your Favorite Animal

Pick your favorite animal and learn more about it! With a grown-up, go online or to your local library to find some facts about your favorite animal.

Write your opinion:

The _____ is my favorite animal

because _____

Write 3 facts you learned about your favorite animal.

1. _____

_____

2. _____

_____

3. _____

_____

Draw a picture of the animal that shows the 3 facts above.

Compare and Contrast: Main Ideas

The platypus is an unusual animal. A platypus has webbed feet and bill, like a duck. Its tail resembles that of a beaver. Its body resembles that of an otter. Males are bigger than females and have sharp, venomous stingers on the heels of their rear feet. The platypus hunts for food underwater. It uses its webbed feet and tail to move around in the water. It eats larvae, insects, shellfish, and worms. Other than being a combination of three different animals, the platypus is one of the only two mammals that lays eggs! (The other is the echidna.) Mammals usually give birth while other animals, such as reptiles and birds, lay eggs. They are commonly found living in the rivers of eastern Australia. They are mainly nocturnal animals, but they can be seen either at night or very early in the morning.

Compare and Contrast: Main Ideas

What is the main idea of this passage? Write your answer in a complete sentence.

List two important details that support the main idea.

1.

2.

Compare and Contrast: Main Ideas

I was fishing very early one morning when I saw something strange. At first, I saw a beaver in the water. I saw its tail as it dove into the water. I didn't think much of it. Then, I saw a duck coming up from the same spot where I saw the beaver. Its duck bill stuck out of the water. As it began to bring its little head out of the water, I saw that it had fur, not feathers! I rubbed my chin and scratched my head. This was the weirdest duck I had ever seen. The sun wasn't fully out yet, so it was a bit dark. I thought maybe it was a beaver after all and my eyes were playing tricks on me. When it stepped out of the water, I saw that it definitely had a bill and even webbed feet like a duck. But then I saw it had four feet instead of two! Its body didn't look like any duck I had ever seen. It was all furry, and it had the same beaver tail I spotted earlier. I wanted to get a closer look, but it quickly burrowed into its home in the ground.

What is the main idea of this passage? Write your answer in a complete sentence.

_____

....

_____
_____

....

_____

List two important details that support the main idea.

1 _____

....

_____
_____

....

_____

2. _____

....

_____
_____

....

_____

Compare and Contrast: Main Ideas

Do you think these two passages are talking about the same animal? Why or why not?

Fairy Tales

classics known and new

2nd GRADE

Table of Contents

Fairy Tales: Classics Known and New

Kasajizo

A Japanese Folktale

This book belongs to:

_____

Once upon a time there was an old man and his wife who were so poor that they were nearly out of rice. It was almost New Year's day and the snow that covered the ground prevented them from gathering materials for weaving hats to sell for money. The mice in their house were hungry too so the old couple gave them the last of their rice.

The mice were so grateful that they gathered materials
for the couple to make hats to sell.

On the way to town, the old man saw stone statues of Ojizo-sama, which are supposed to protect the people in the town. The old man noticed that their heads were covered in snow so he gently brushed the snow away.

He continued to town to sell his hats but no one bought any. He was disappointed and started to walk home. As he came upon the Ojizo-sama statues, he felt badly for not having something to give to them. Seeing that their heads were covered again in snow he decided to give the Ojizo-sama statues his hats.

The man returned home empty handed and told his wife and the mice what happened. They all agreed that it was a kind thing to do. Just then, they heard voices outside yelling, "Happy New Year!" They ran outside to see the Ojizo-sama statues with a sleigh full of food. The old man, his wife and the mice shared the food and celebrated the New Year.

TREASURE ISLAND

Jim Hawkins meets Billy Bones who secretly tells him about the famous Captain Flint and his buried treasure. Bones warns him of a one-legged man.

TREASURE ISLAND

Blind Pew, an old crewmate of Bones', appears and fights Bones to get the map to Captain Flint's buried treasure.

TREASURE ISLAND

Pirates attack the Hawkins' inn looking for Bones and the treasure map. However, Jim has already run away with the map.

TREASURE ISLAND

Jim takes the map to Dr. Livesey. He, Squire Trelawney and Jim examine the map together. It shows the detailed location of Flint's treasure. Trelawney immediatly wants to hunt the treasure down so they buy a ship and hire a crew.

TREASURE ISLAND

Jim meets Long John Silver, the ship cook. Long John Silver helps Trelawney hire the rest of the ship's crew.

TREASURE ISLAND

While onboard, Jim overhears some
of the crew planning a mutiny
to take the treasure.

TREASURE ISLAND

When they reach Treasure Island most of Long John Silver's mutinous men go ashore first. Jim runs away and meets Ben Gunn. Ben Gunn had been left on the island by Captain Flint.

TREASURE ISLAND

Trelawney, Dr. Livesey and their men overpower the remaining pirates on the ship. But one pirate attacks Jim in the rigging.

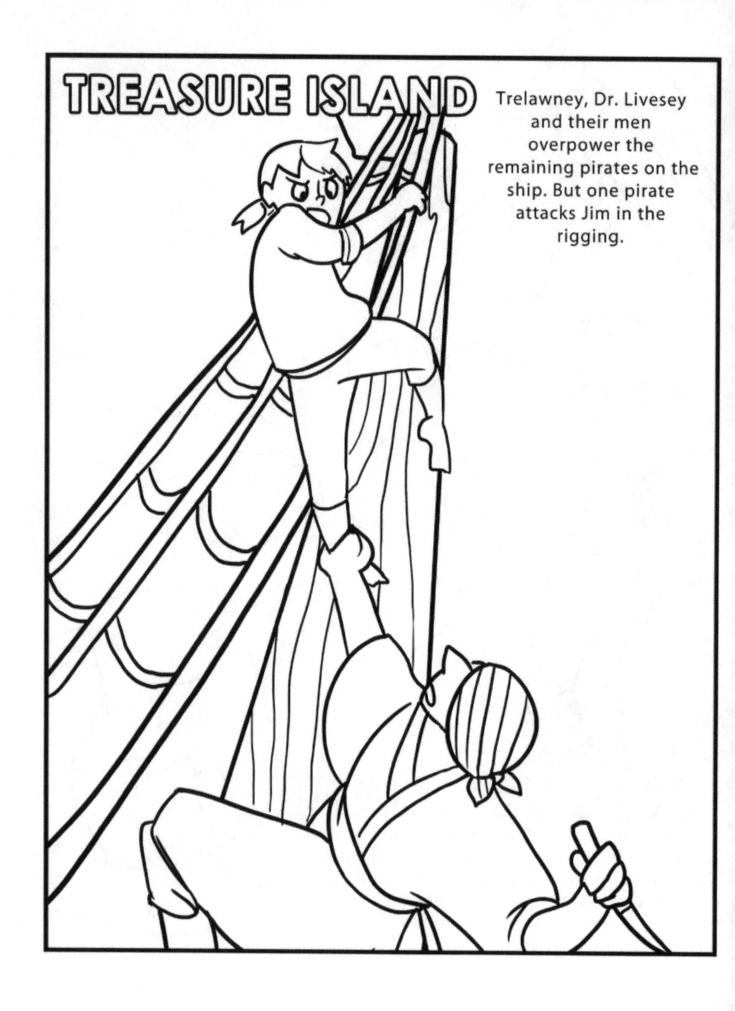

TREASURE ISLAND

Silver's men want to overthrow him so he
uses Jim to read the map to get to where
the treasure is.

TREASURE ISLAND

Jim leads them to the treasure only to find that it has already been taken. There the pirates are ambushed by Dr. Livesey, Trelawney and their men.

TREASURE ISLAND

They go to Ben Gunn's cave where Gunn has hidden the treasure for months. It is divided with the loyal crew members and they leave the pirates on the island.

TREASURE ISLAND   Silver escapes with a small part of the treasure.

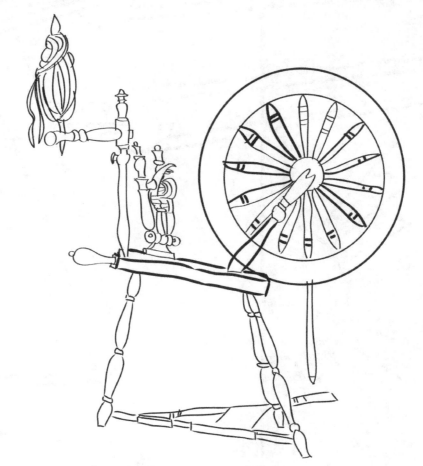

Briar Rose

by

The Brothers Grimm

There was once a king and queen who very much wanted
a child. The king was very proud when his daughter
Briar Rose was born.

The King decided to hold a banquet so all could see the child.
At the feast 12 good fairies came to bestow a wish on her. One gave
beauty, one gave the gift of song and one of kindness,
and so on.

But a 13th fairy, who was mean and evil, felt left out. So she cursed Briar Rose, saying, "She shall die after touching a spinning wheel." The last fairy had not given her gift. To save the girl she cast a spell that would make her sleep for 100 years instead.

Briar Rose did grow in grace and beauty, but the one spell
the good fairies left out was curiosity. Briar loved to go
about the castle and into the forest to
explore and find new things.

On the morning of Briar Rose's birthday she found at the tip
most top tower was the mean fairy spinning wool. She
could not help herself and touched the sharp
spindle and fell instantly asleep.

The sleep spell that spared Briar Rose life also put everyone in the castle to sleep.

It was many years until a knight came to the castle. A few good fairies told him that in the highest tower was a beautiful sleeping princess waiting to be awoken by him.

The good knight was so shocked by Briar Rose's beauty,
he could not stop himself from kissing her.

Then the castle came back to life! The king and queen
were so happy, they decided the brave knight
could marry the beautiful Briar Rose.
The End.

There was once a velveteen rabbit, and in the beginning he was really splendid. He was fat and bunchy, as a rabbit should be; his coat was spotted brown and white, he had real thread whiskers, and his ears were lined with pink sateen. On Christmas morning, when he sat wedged in the top of the Boy's stocking, with a sprig of holly between his paws, the effect was charming.

For a long time he lived in the toy cupboard or on the nursery floor, and no
one thought very much about him. He
was naturally shy, and being only made
of velveteen, some of the more expensive
toys quite snubbed him. The mechanical
toys were very superior, and looked
down upon every one else; they were full
of modern ideas, and pretended they
were real.

The Skin Horse had lived longer in the nursery than any of the others. He was so old that his brown coat was bald in patches and showed the seams underneath, and most of the hairs in his tail had been pulled out to string bead necklaces. He was wise, for he had seen a long succession of mechanical toys arrive to boast and swagger, and by-and-by break their mainsprings and pass away, and he knew that they were only toys, and would never turn into anything else. For nursery magic is very strange and wonderful, and only those playthings that are old and wise and experienced like the Skin Horse understand all about it.

One evening, when the Boy was going to bed, he couldn't find the china dog that always slept with him. Nana was in a hurry, and it was too much trouble to hunt for china dogs at bedtime, so she simply looked about her, and seeing that the toy cupboard door stood open, she made a swoop.

"Here," she said, "take your old Bunny! He'll do to sleep with you!" And she dragged the Rabbit out by one ear, and put him into the Boy's arms.

And so time went on, and the little Rabbit was very happy—so happy that he never noticed how his beautiful velveteen fur was getting shabbier and shabbier, and his tail becoming unsewn, and all the pink rubbed off his nose where the Boy had kissed him.

Spring came, and they had long days in the garden, for wherever the Boy went the Rabbit went too. He had rides in the wheelbarrow, and picnics on the grass, and lovely fairy huts built for him under the raspberry canes behind the flower border.

One evening, while the Rabbit was lying there alone, watching the ants that ran to and fro between his velvet paws in the grass, he saw two strange beings creep out of the tall bracken near him.

They were rabbits like himself, but quite furry and brand-new. They must have been very well made, for their seams didn't show at all, and they changed shape in a queer way when they moved; one minute they were long and thin and the next minute fat and bunchy, instead of always staying the same like he did.

Weeks passed, and the little Rabbit grew very old and shabby, but the Boy loved him just as much. He loved him so hard that he loved all his whiskers off, and the pink lining to his ears turned grey, and his brown spots faded. He even began to lose his shape, and he scarcely looked like a rabbit any more, except to the Boy. To him he was always beautiful, and that was all that the little Rabbit cared about. He didn't mind how he looked to other people, because the nursery magic had made him Real, and when you are Real shabbiness doesn't matter.

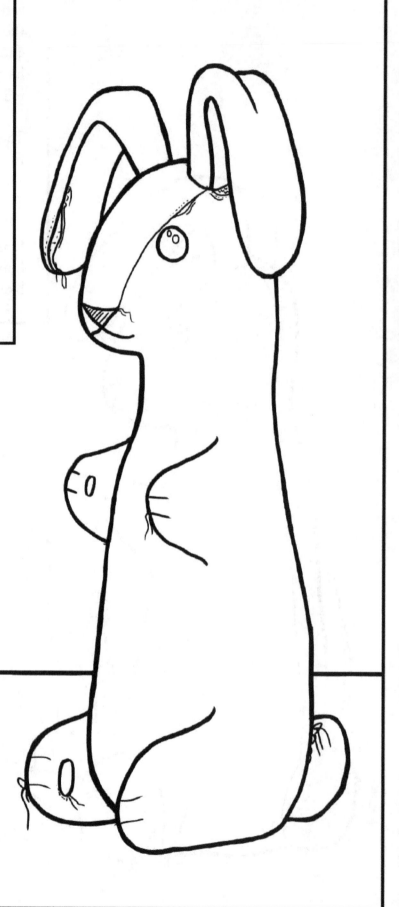

And then, one day, the Boy was ill.

His face grew very flushed, and he talked in his sleep, and his little body was so hot that it burned the Rabbit when he held him close. Strange people came and went in the nursery, and a light burned all night and through it all the little Velveteen Rabbit lay there, hidden from sight under the bedclothes, and he never stirred, for he was afraid that if they found him some one might take him away, and he knew that the Boy needed him.

"How about his old Bunny?" she asked.

"That?" said the doctor. "Why, it's a mass of scarlet fever germs!—Burn it at once. What? Nonsense! Get him a new one. He mustn't have that any more!"

And so the little Rabbit was put into a sack with the old picture-books and a lot of rubbish, and carried out to the end of the garden behind the fowl-house. That was a fine place to make a bonfire, only the gardener was too busy just then to attend to it. He had the potatoes to dig and the green peas to gather, but next morning he promised to come quite early and burn the whole lot.

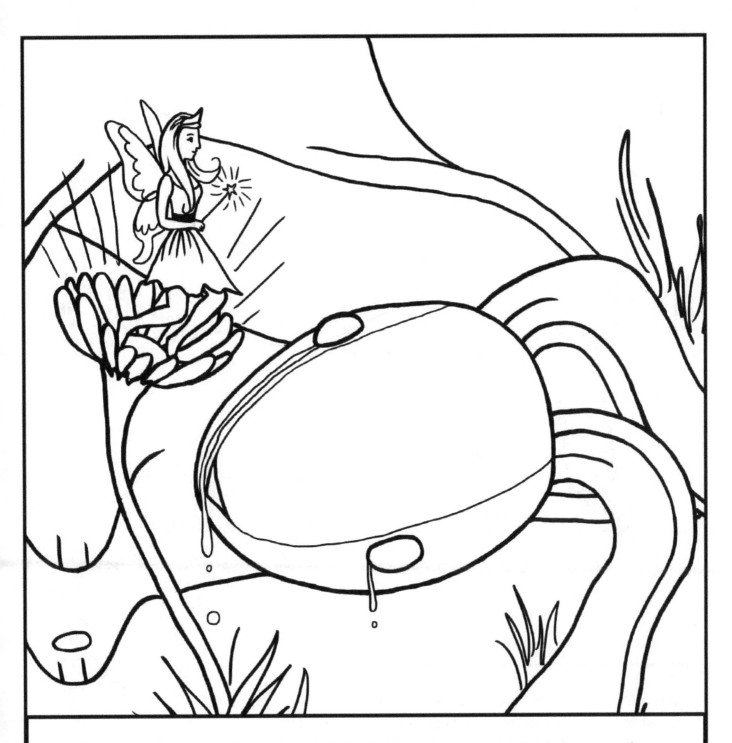

And a tear, a real tear, trickled down his little shabby velvet nose and fell to the ground.

And then a strange thing happened. For where the tear had fallen a flower grew out of the ground, a mysterious flower, not at all like any that grew in the garden. It had slender green leaves the color of emeralds, and in the centre of the leaves a blossom like a golden cup. It was so beautiful that the little Rabbit forgot to cry, and just lay there watching it. And presently the blossom opened, and out of it there stepped a fairy.

"You were Real to the Boy," the Fairy said, "because he loved you. Now you shall be Real to every one."

It was light now, for the moon had risen. All the
forest was beautiful, and the fronds of the
bracken shone like frosted silver. In the open
glade between the tree-trunks the wild rabbits
danced with their shadows on the velvet grass,
but when they saw the Fairy they all stopped
dancing and stood round in a ring to stare at her.

"I've brought you a new playfellow," the Fairy
said. "You must be very kind to him and teach
him all he needs to know in Rabbit-land, for he
is going to live with you for ever and ever!"

Reading
Treasure Chest

2nd GRADE

Meet Captain Hook, Blackbeard, and his mates and join them in their adventures!

education.com

Table of Contents

Reading Treasure Chest

This is Captain Hook. He is the mean pirate captain of The Jolly Roger and the lord of the pirate village in Neverland. He wears a hook in place of his right hand, which was cut off by his archenemy Peter Pan, who fed it to a crocodile! Many fear Captain Hook...except, of course, for brave Peter Pan!

Ahoy there matey! This is Blackbeard, the most feared and notorious of all pirates in the 18th century! A shrewd and calculating leader, Blackbeard used his fearsome image to scare those he desired to steal from. He even lit fuses under his hat to frighten his enemies!

Young William Kidd became a captain on the day a ship's crew mutinied! He was appointed captain and the ship was re-named the Blessed William. After proving to be good at protecting British colonies from the French, he spent some time as a privateer – someone who worked for a country's government to attack foreign shipping in a time of war.

Captain Kidd was hired by rich men to set sail for the Indian Ocean to hunt for pirates and rogues who were enemies of England. Making a ship ready to sail with supplies, crewmen and repairs was expensive to do, but the possibility of treasure was appealing. Any treasure Captain Kidd found he only had to share some of it with the men who'd hired him. On the ship the Adventure Galley, he found himself in trouble almost as soon as he set sail from London. When a ship of the Royal Navy was passing by, Captain Kidd and his crew refused to salute. As punishment for this (very pirate-like) behavior the navy held most of his crew. This forced him to hire new crewmen in other ports along the way.

By the time Captain Kidd reached the Indian Ocean he was running out of time! He had not found any pirates, his crew was getting sick, and his ship was breaking down! Captain Kidd made a decision: they would attack any ship that passed by, in hopes of finding treasure. It was one year past the date he was supposed to return to England with loot. If he didn't find any, he'd be in a lot of trouble.

An Armenian ship, called the Cara Merchant, came within view full of expensive fabrics, gold and silver. There were no pirates on that ship but Kidd captured it and took the ship and all its treasures. He sold the goods for profit and hid the Cara Merchant, anchored off of an island in the Caribbean.

Captain Kidd was captured. He owed men in England a lot of money and he'd stolen a ship! But before he was captured he buried his treasure; no one knows where. Some people say that to this day his treasure is there, buried somewhere in the Caribbean.

Blackbeard was a fierce pirate. He started his career as a privateer, but soon carved his own path on the waters in true pirate-style. His ship was called Queen Anne's Revenge. He spent most of his pirate life sailing up and down the eastern coast of the Americas and the Caribbean.

Blackbeard's most daring exploit was in May of 1718. Using Queen Anne's Revenge and two other ships, Blackbeard blocked the harbor of Charleston, South Carolina, keeping any ships from leaving or entering. He pillaged a couple of vessels for valuables on-board. And he took a number of the city's important citizens as hostages for ransom. His only ransom demand: a chest full of medicine.

When the demands were met, Blackbeard released the hostages and left Charleston harbor without having fired any shots.

PIRATE PUPPET

1. COLOR IN THE PIRATE.
2. CUT OUT THE PIRATE PARTS BY CUTTING AROUND THE BOLD LINES.
3. USE PAPER FASTENERS TO CONNECT THE PARTS TO THEIR MATCHING LETTERS. LETTERS WITH CIRCLES ON THEM GO ON TOP WHILE CIRCLE-LESS LETTERS GO BELOW.

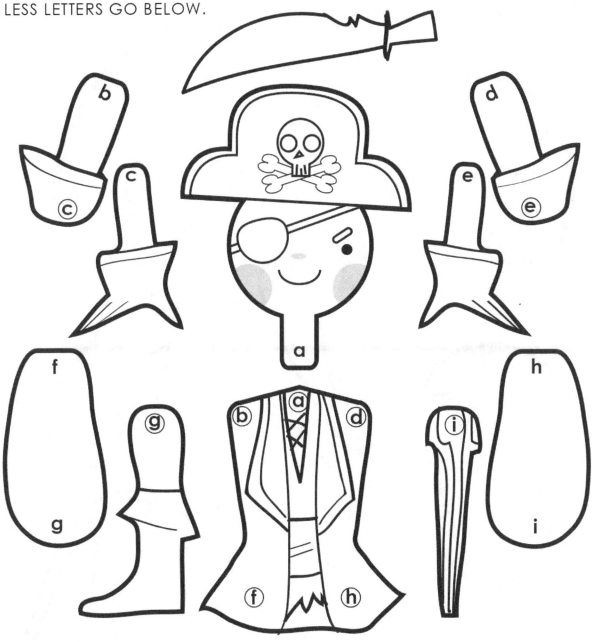

MERMAID PUPPET

1. COLOR IN THE MERMAID.
2. CUT OUT EACH PART BY CUTTING AROUND THE BOLD LINES.
3. MATCH THE LETTERS AND CONNECT THE PARTS USING PAPER FASTENERS. LETTERS WITH CIRCLES ON THEM GO ON TOP WHILE CIRCLELESS LETTERS GO BELOW.

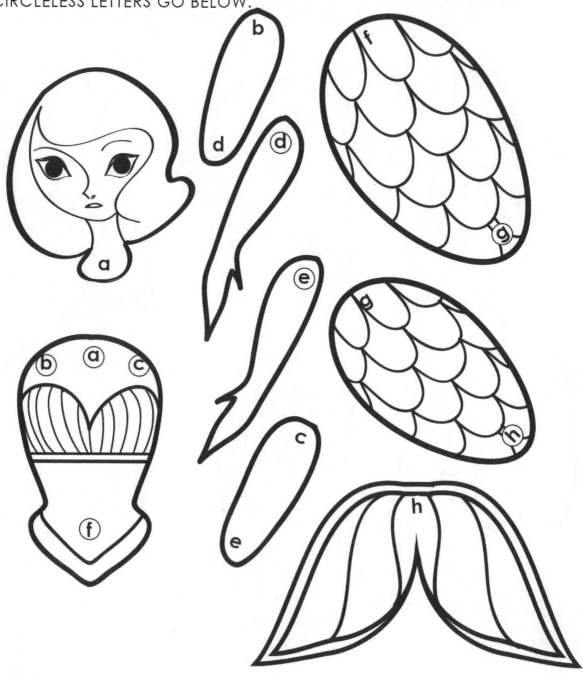

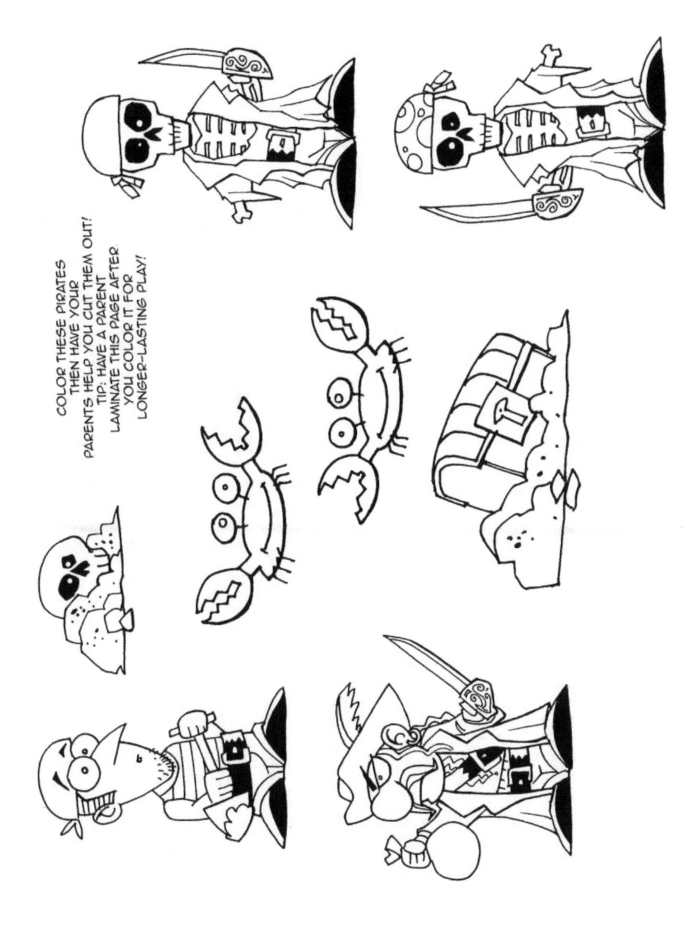

COLOR THESE PIRATES
THEN HAVE YOUR
PARENTS HELP YOU CUT THEM OUT!
TIP: HAVE A PARENT
LAMINATE THIS PAGE AFTER
YOU COLOR IT FOR
LONGER-LASTING PLAY!

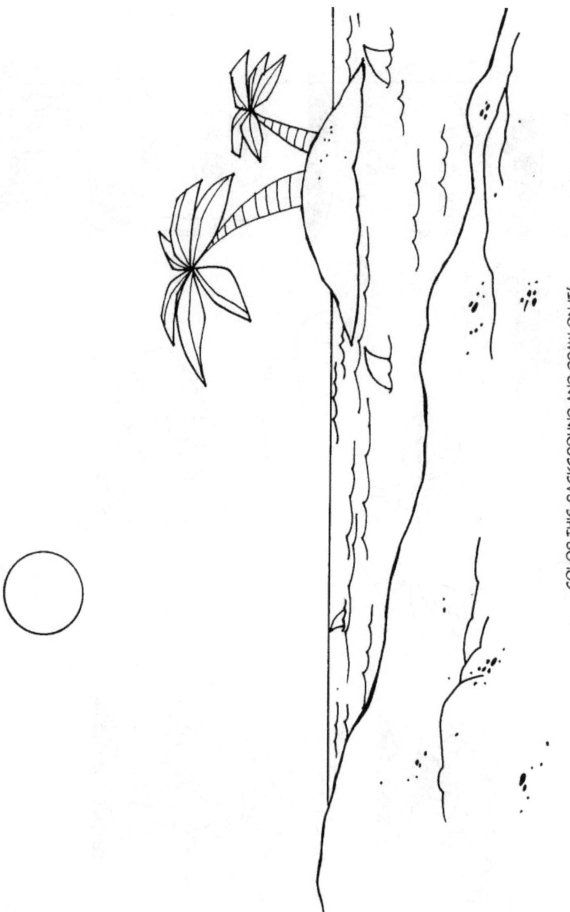

COLOR THIS BACKGROUND AND DRAW ON IT!

TIP: HAVE A PARENT LAMINATE THIS PAGE AFTER YOU COLOR IT FOR LONGER-LASTING PLAY!

TREASURE MAP

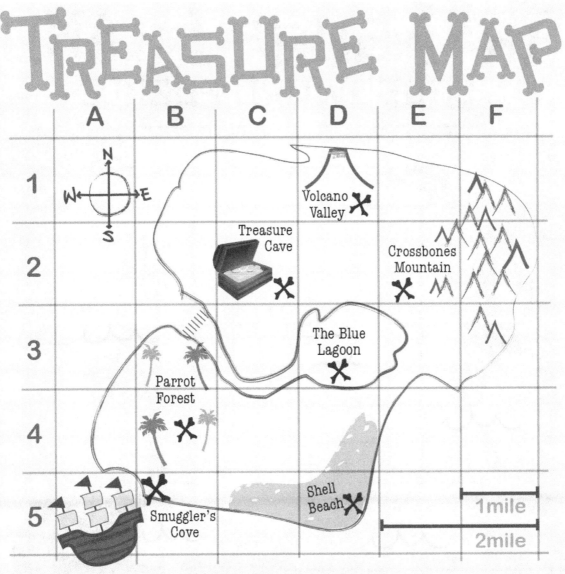

YOU HAVE LANDED ON TREASURE ISLAND. Each landmark on the map lies within a square that's named after the column and row that make its sides. For Example, you have landed on Smugglers Cove. It is located under column B row 5, which meants it is in square B5. Fill out the location of the other landmarks below.

Parrot Forest _____ _____   The Blue Lagoon _____ _____

Volcano Valley _____   Crossbones Mountain _____ _____ _____ _____

Shell Beach _____ _____ _____   Treasure Cave _____

TREASURE ISLAND
CROSSWORD PUZZLE

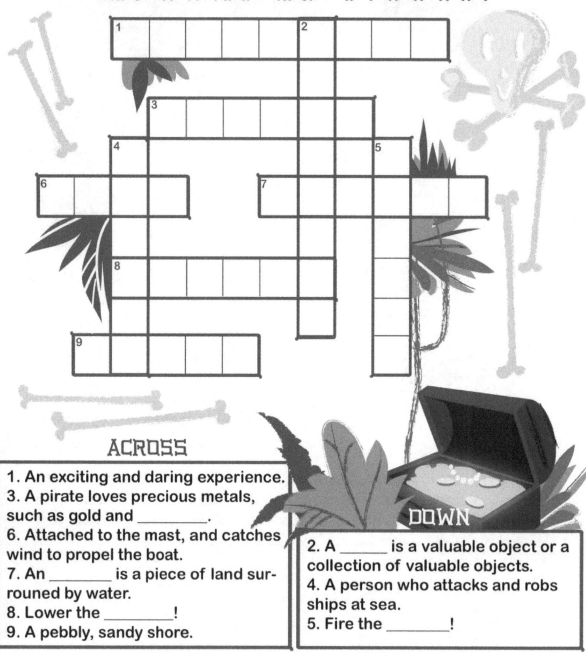

ACROSS

1. An exciting and daring experience.
3. A pirate loves precious metals, such as gold and _____.
6. Attached to the mast, and catches wind to propel the boat.
7. An _____ is a piece of land surrouned by water.
8. Lower the _____!
9. A pebbly, sandy shore.

DOWN

2. A _____ is a valuable object or a collection of valuable objects.
4. A person who attacks and robs ships at sea.
5. Fire the _____!

WORD BOX

ISLAND/TREASURE/SAIL/CANNON/ANCHOR
WIND/ADVENTURE /PIRATES/SILVER/BEACH

Vocabulary
in focus

2nd GRADE

HOMOPHONES

sea see
weight wait
cent sent
made maid
pear pair

hair	brush	**COMPOUND WORDS**
paint		
tooth		

Table of Contents

Vocabulary in Focus

Same Sounds

Circle the correct **homophone** to complete the sentence.

Homophones are words that sound the same but have different spellings and meanings.

1. I just (eight / ate) a lot of (meat / meet) for dinner.

2. I can't (wait / weight) to receive your letter in the (male / mail)!

3. My mom bought (two / to) pounds of delicious (beats / beets).

4. Jack is spending the (weak / week) with his (aunt / ant).

5. We (won / one) (hour / our) first basketball game!

6. Would you like to (where / wear) a (pear / pair) of my mittens?

7. Mr. Smith's (son / sun) is an (I / eye) doctor.

8. (Their / There) is an (acts / ax) over by the tree.

Simone's Homophones

Simone is an excellent speller, but she tends to get confused when two words sound similar. Help Simone write what she means by underlining each incorrect homophone and writing the correct word on the lines given.

I walked inn to the pet store because their was a sign that said "Puppies for sail." The cutest one had a short tail and white pause.

_____ _____ _____ _____

When I'm board and my mom isn't home, I like two try on her high healed shoes. There difficult to ware, but they make me three inches taller.

_____ _____ _____

My cousin Julius scent me a postcard in the male. He is at the beach in Hawaii with his knew surfboard. He has been surfing four over twenty years.

_____

_____

_____

_____

I can't weight for softball season this year. My too favorite positions to play are write field and third bass.

_____

_____

_____

_____

Check The Homophones #1

Homophones are words that sound alike, but have different meanings.
Fix the sentences below by circling the incorrect homophone and
writing the correct one in the space.

I didn't (sea) any squirrels at the park.

see

I can't weight for my friend to call back.

I cent Roy a present for his birthday.

John's made washes his clothes.

Yesterday I war my favorite skirt to school.

Watch out for bares!

He bought a new pear of jeans.

Check The Homophones #2

Homophones are words that sound alike, but have different meanings.
Fix the sentences below by circling the incorrect homophone and
writing the right one in the space.

My arm is (soar.)

sore

I ate a pair for lunch today.

Kids love reading fairy tails.

Jimmy had serial for breakfast.

Sally ate a turkey sandwich on wheat bred.

This sock has a whole.

Pick The Homophones #1

Homophones are words that sound alike, but have different meanings.
Complete each sentence using a homophone from the word bank.

whether	by	heal
where	tail	tale	wear
heel	buy	weather

Isabel wants the new book [ ] her favorite author. Her mom promised to [ ] it for her.

I hurt my [ ]. The doctor told me it will take 2 weeks to [ ].

I love parties [ ] people [ ] costumes.

[ ] I go to the gym or jog outside depends on the [ ].

I wrote a [ ] about a dragon with a long, green [ ].

Pick The Homophones #2

Homophones are words that sound alike, but have different meanings.
Complete each sentence using a homophone from the word bank.

sent

fair

son

sun   see   weigh

fare

sea   way   cent

Farmer John and his [   ] get up before the [   ] rises.

I [   ] my friend a postcard that cost 1 [   ] .

The [   ] for the street [   ] is cheap.

The [   ] is so clear that you can [   ] the fish.

These hamburgers [   ] 5 pounds. There's no [   ] I can eat them all!

These three words sound the same, but they all have different meanings!
- Buy is a verb. *You can buy a ticket at the counter.*
- By is a preposition. *I saw a squirrel by the tree.*
- Bye is short for "goodbye."

Complete each sentence with the correct homophone: buy, by, or bye.

Where did you _____ your dress? It's very cute!

_____ the way, have you tried the new frozen yogurt?

I like to _____ popcorn at the zoo.

She knows the song _____ heart.

Do you see the girl sitting _____ Tommy?

_____ ! See you again soon.

I watched the train pass _____ .

I want to _____ a new camera.

It's or Its

It's and its sound the same, but they have different meanings!
- Its is a possessive pronoun. *The dog plays with its tail.*
- It's is a contraction meaning "it is."

Complete the sentences with the correct homophone: it's or its.

The bird picked up a worm with [ ] beak.

[ ] time for dinner!

My mom thinks [ ] good to learn how to swim.

A crocodile uses [ ] long tail for swimming.

I want to play in the snow, but [ ] too cold.

The dolphin uses [ ] fin to control [ ] direction.

Who's Or Whose

Who's and whose sound the same, but they have different meanings!
- Whose is a possessive pronoun. *Whose dog is it?*
- Who's is a contraction meaning "who is."

Complete the sentences with the correct homophone: who's or whose.

[ ] car is parked in the driveway?

I know the kid [ ] bike is red.

Aunt Marie is a person [ ] kind and cheerful.

[ ] shoes are in the hallway?

I think I know [ ] making that squeaky sound.

This party is awesome! [ ] idea was it?

Tommy is a boy [ ] dog can play cool tricks.

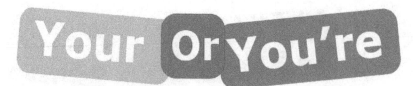

Your Or You're

Your and you're sound the same, but they have different meanings!
- Your is a possessive pronoun. *Your sister is pretty.*
- You're is a contraction meaning "you are."

Complete the sentences with the correct homophone: your or you're.

Getting lots of sleep is good for [ ] health.

[ ] house is across the street from mine.

Don't forget to bring [ ] lunch box to school.

If [ ] feeling sick, you should go to bed.

When [ ] sad, you want to cry.

[ ] happy because it's your birthday.

The sign says "Please clean up after [ ] meal".

Wow! [ ] wearing [ ] diamond ring.

Their Or They're

Their and they're sound the same, but they have different meanings!
- Their is a possessive pronoun. *Their house is red.*
- They're is a contraction meaning "they are."

Complete the sentences with the correct homophone: their or they're.

The graduates received _____ diplomas.

These toads are jumping high because _____ happy.

The married couple put _____ pictures on the wall.

The chicks always follow _____ mother.

I love puppies because _____ small and fluffy.

The twins are not allow to drive the car because _____ too young.

I love to eat at Sushi House because _____ food is yummy!

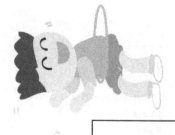

A Brief History of the Hula Hoop

Look at the timeline below and answer the questions.

1000 BC
Greeks make hoops out of grape leaves.

1300
Hooping becomes popular in Great Britain.

1800
British sailors see hula dancing on the Hawaiian Islands and rename the activity "Hula Hooping".

1958
Richard Knerr and Arthur "Spud" Melin start mass manufacturing hula hoops out of plastic.

Timeline markers: 1000 BC, 1300, 1800, 1900, 2000, 2010

In 1000 BC, what material did Greeks use to make hoops?

What happened in Great Britain in 1300?

Where did British sailors see hula dancing?

What did Richard Knerr and Arthur "Spud" Melin do?

A Brief History of Bubble Gum

Look at the timeline below and answer the questions.

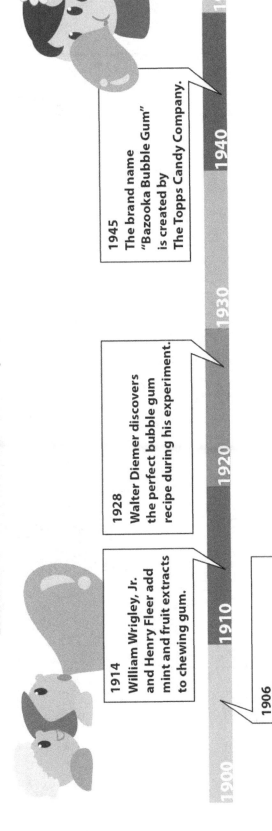

1914
William Wrigley, Jr.
and Henry Fleer add
mint and fruit extracts
to chewing gum.

1928
Walter Diemer discovers
the perfect bubble gum
recipe during his experiment.

1945
The brand name
"Bazooka Bubble Gum"
is created by
The Topps Candy Company.

1906
Frank Fleer tries to make
bubble gum but it is
very sticky.

1900   1910   1920   1930   1940   1950

Whose bubble gum was too sticky?

_____

In what year was the perfect bubble gum discovered?

_____

Who discovered the perfect bubble gum?

_____

What brand of bubble gum was created
in 1945?

_____

The **Ozark Big-Eared Bat** can be found in the Ozark Mountains
of Arkansas, Missouri and Oklahoma. This bat's ears are more
than a quarter the length of its body. During hibernation, some
big-eared bats curl their ears up like a ram's horns.

Synonym Match!

Match each word to its **synonym**.

Synonyms are words that have the same or almost the same meaning.

big	speedy
pretty	little
happy	large
small	damp
fast	begin
start	glad
also	beautiful
wet	too

Plural Practice 1

Draw a line to match the picture to the correct spelling of the singular or plural form.

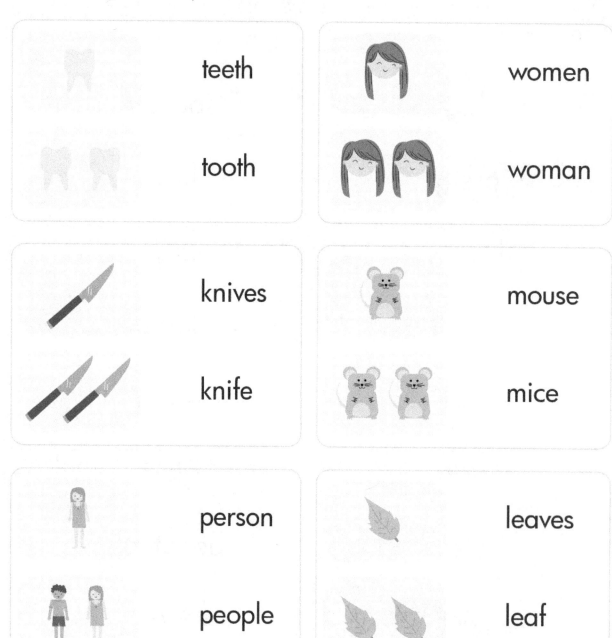

teeth

tooth

women

woman

knives

knife

mouse

mice

person

people

leaves

leaf

Plural Practice 2

Draw a line to match the picture to the correct spelling of the singular or plural form.

child

children

elf

elves

wolf

wolves

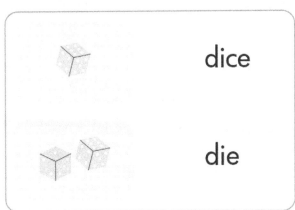

dice

die

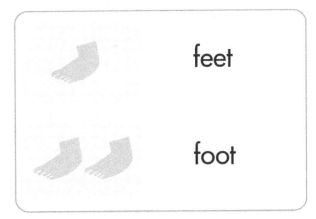

feet

foot

goose

geese

Words Ending in Y

All of the words in the word box end in **y**.
If the y word has a **long e** sound, like **baby**,
write the word under the baby.
If the y word has a **long i** sound, like **spy**,
write the word under the spy.

bunny	very	my	sky	happy
fly	cry	shiny	penny	shy

baby

_____

_____

_____

_____

spy

_____

_____

_____

_____

Shh ... Silent Letters

All of these words have silent letters.
Say and rewrite each word. Circle the silent letter or letters.

knee   _____

sigh   _____

write   _____

climb   _____

thumb   _____

who   _____

high   _____

lamb   _____

Silent Letters Crossword

Use the clues to complete the crossword.
All of the answers are words with silent letters.

Across

1. I am a stop _____. **STOP**

3. I can help you untangle your hair.

6. I can help you cut your vegetables.

7. I can be difficult to untie.

Down

2. I live in a garden and wear a pointed hat.

4. I can explode!

5. I carry a sword and live in a castle.

Reading
Vocabulary

LET'S GO CAMPING! VOCABULARY

Camping is a fun outdoor activity that provides a chance to explore nature, go hiking, eat over a campfire, stargaze, and sleep in a tent. Watch out for bears as you search for the camping words below! They're spelled forwards, and up and down.

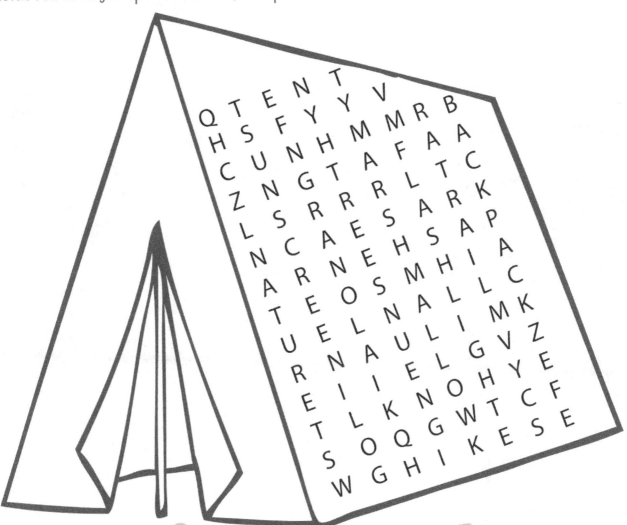

 tent

nature

 sunscreen

backpack

hike

 trees

log

flashlight

trail

 marshmallow

granola

What is your favorite camping activity?

Down On The Farm

Find the names of your favorite things that you can find on a farm in the word search below. They may be written forward, backward, horizontally, vertically, or even diagonally!

When you are done with your word search, color the farm animals!

chicken
cow
farm
dirt
hill
horse
pig
sheep
sun
tree

l	o	k	d	s	m	r	a	f	g
a	d	f	s	u	n	h	j	c	k
d	i	z	x	c	v	b	h	m	l
w	r	c	t	u	y	i	o	r	g
q	t	a	r	s	c	d	r	f	i
z	n	l	e	k	j	h	s	g	p
x	d	c	e	v	b	n	e	m	l
u	b	n	j	g	h	x	w	o	c
o	e	a	u	p	e	e	h	s	i
h	i	l	l	w	a	g	j	p	x

Find the Plural!

Write the plural for each word by adding s or es.
Circle the plural forms in the word search.

A	P	E	N	S	A	N	H
D	Y	E	T	G	L	B	I
B	U	S	E	S	A	O	C
O	S	N	F	X	K	A	D
X	B	C	A	T	S	T	V
E	P	L	O	C	A	S	E
S	G	L	A	S	S	E	S
A	H	E	B	I	J	D	W

cat _____

box _____

boat _____   glass _____

bus _____   pen_____

Word Search ROAD TRIP

There are 19 words hidden in the word search below.
Circle the words as you find them and then cross
each one off the list below the puzzle.

```
C A V S E S S A L G N U S R
T R A F F I C O X Y N E O E
A Z C E N I D Y L O F A K A
S P A R A Z J I I H D S U H
I O T C A O E T N L E T O M
G K I R E C A R S E A T S E
H N O R K N L P P W R H T S
T U N G I F S N G I S E R A
S R G T M L R M S N E K E C
E T S B G E P E T D M A E T
E E T R A V E L E O T S T I
D R E S R M I O T W A O E U
Y A W H G I H E A M A I A S
S E A T B E L T S R I Y R K
```

VACATION   SIGNS   SIGHTSEE   TRAVEL   SUITCASE
DINER   ROAD   CAR   SEATBELTS   SUNGLASSES
WINDOW   HIGHWAY   TRAFFIC   DESTINATION
CARSEAT   MOTEL   FREEWAY   TRUNK   STREET

WORDPLAY PUZZLER 1

Look at each list of 3 words. They might not seem to belong in the
same set or category, but don't let the pictures fool you!
Find the one word that ties them all together.
For example, **hair**, **paint** and **tooth** all describe a kind of **brush**.
(hairbrush, paintbrush and toothbrush.)

		example
	hair	**brush**
	paint	
	tooth	

		4.
	foot	
	beach	
	basket	

		1.
	pan	
	cheese	
	cup	

		5.
	book	
	earth	
	inch	

		2.
	butter	
	house	
	fire	

		6.
	clown	
	cat	
	shell	

		3.
	tree	
	club	
	bird	

		7.
	sun	
	bird	
	bubble	

WORDPLAY PUZZLER 2

Look at each list of 3 words. They might not seem to belong in the
same set or category, but don't let the pictures fool you!
Find the one word that ties them all together.
For example, **hair**, **paint** and **tooth** all describe a kind of **brush**.
(hairbrush, paintbrush and toothbrush.)

		example
	hair	
	paint	**brush**
	tooth	

		4.
	lip	
	walking	
	drum	

		1.
	note	
	cook	
	phone	

		5.
	baseball	
	bottle	
	skull	

		2.
	head	
	sun	
	night	

		6.
	onion	
	ear	
	diamond	

		3.
	flower	
	river	
	feather	

		7.
	stair	
	suit	
	book	

answers : 1. book 2. light 3. bed 4. stick 5. cap 6. ring 7. case

Presidential
Puzzler

2nd GRADE

Table of Contents

Presidential Puzzler

WASHINGTON DC
symbols

Washington, D.C. is our nation's capitol, and it's full of interesting things to see! Join the Mack family as they tour this great city.

Bonus Activity: Use your creativity to color in the illustrations!

SCARLETT OAK:
This is the official tree of Washington, D.C.

WASHINGTON MONUMENT
This monument was completed in 1884, and it is a tribute to the first U.S. president, George Washington. It is 555 feet tall.

The scarlett oak leaf turns vibrant red during the autumn season!

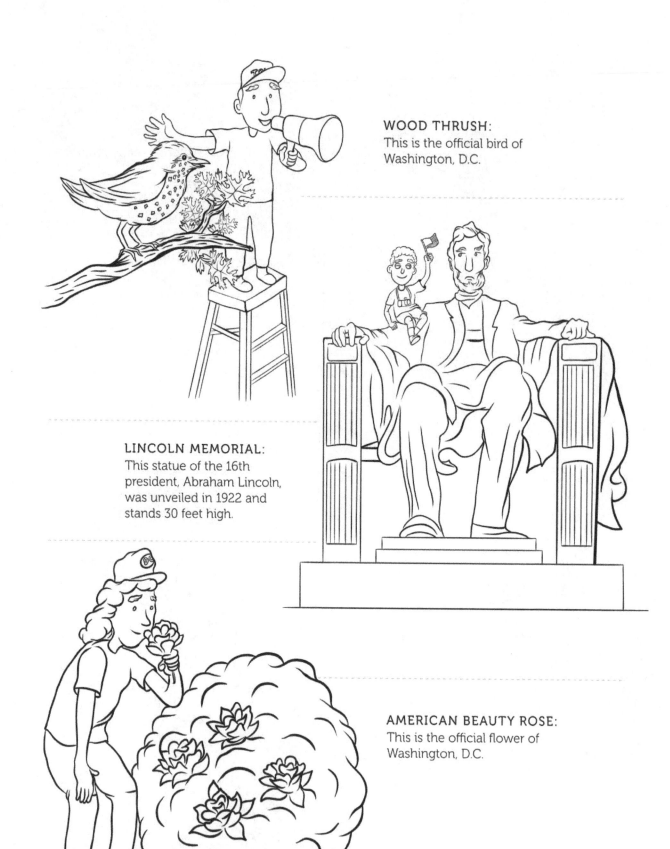

WOOD THRUSH:
This is the official bird of Washington, D.C.

LINCOLN MEMORIAL:
This statue of the 16th president, Abraham Lincoln, was unveiled in 1922 and stands 30 feet high.

AMERICAN BEAUTY ROSE:
This is the official flower of Washington, D.C.

Presidential

SEAL

The Seal of the President of the United States is a symbol for the presidency. It is used on presidential vehicles, podiums, and documents from the president to Congress.

The eagle stands for liberty. The arrows represent strength in unity. The olive branch is a symbol of peace. There are 13 stripes and 13 stars, which stand for the thirteen colonies. The motto, "E pluribus unum," is Latin for "Many uniting into one."

example

1 - Light Yellow   4 - Red   7 - Brown

2 - Gold or Yellow   5 - Bright Blue

3 - Dark Blue   6 - Green

THE
United States
FLAG

The United States has 13 stripes for the 13 colonies, which became the first 13 states. It has 50 stars for the 50 states.

The American flag is displayed outside many public buildings, such as libraries, courthouses, police stations, and city halls.

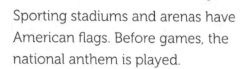

Sporting stadiums and arenas have American flags. Before games, the national anthem is played.

Neil Armstrong was the first man to set foot on the moon in 1969, and he raised an American flag there.

Many people display the American flag outside their homes, especially on civic holidays, such as 4th of July, Memorial Day, Veterans Day, Presidents Day, and Labor Day.

Many schools display the American flag.

Executive Branch:

The president leads the executive branch, carrying out laws, vetoing laws, directing national defense, and directing government. This branch works in the White House.

Judicial Branch:

The Supreme Court, made of nine judges, leads the Judicial Branch. This branch reviews laws and decides cases that involve states' rights. This branch works in the Supreme Court Building.

Legislative Branch:

The House of Representatives includes 435 voting members, and the Senate includes 100 people. These people make up Congress, and they lead the legislative branch. They make laws, then send them to the president for approval. This branch works in the United States Capitol.

The WHITE HOUSE

George Washington was sworn in as our first president in the county's first capital, New York City. He decided to move the capital to its current location and named it the District of Columbia for Christopher Columbus. George Washington never lived in the White House. It wasn't built in time. The first president to live in the White House was John Adams, the second president of the United States.

PRESIDENTIAL MAZE

The president needs to get back to the White House pronto! Help the confused Secret Servicemen lead the president back home safely.

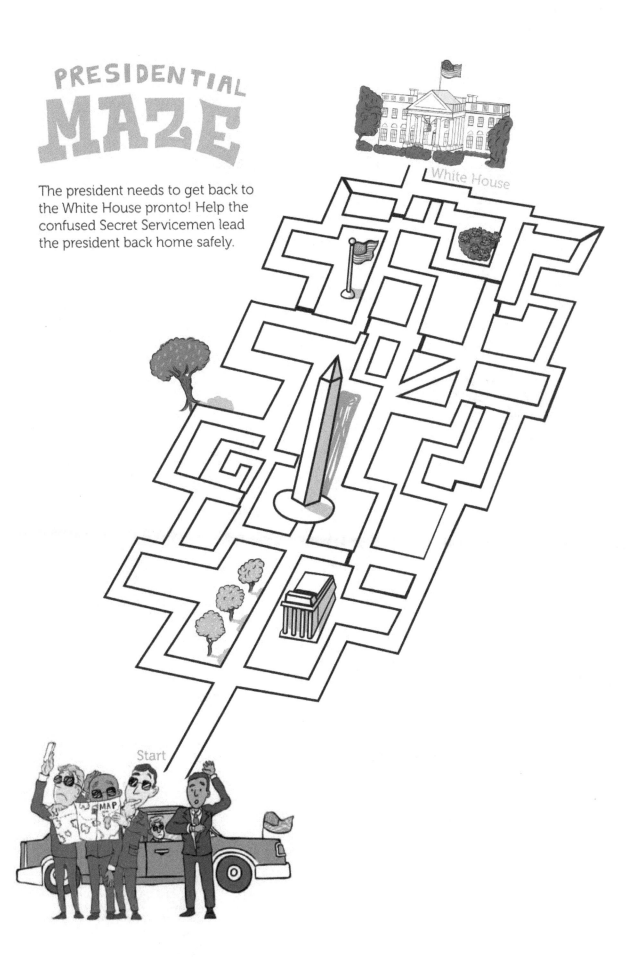

White House

Start

WASHINGTON D.C.

DOT 2 DOT

Skip count by two to connect the dots.

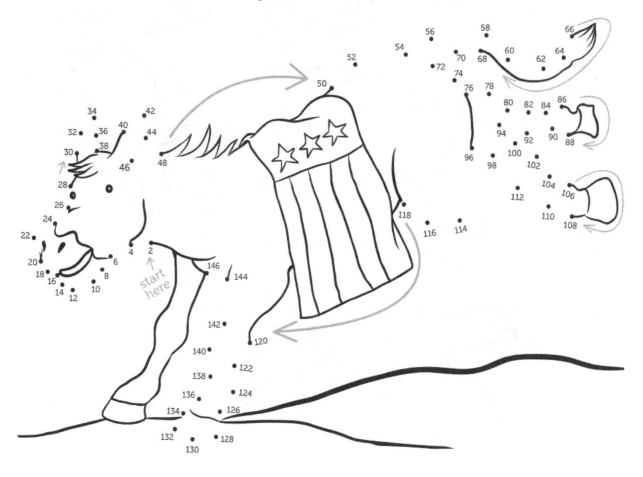

This animal is the unofficial symbol of
the Democratic Party of the United States.

What is this animal? ....

Bonus Activity: Color in the drawing after connecting the dots.

WASHINGTON D.C.

DOT 2 DOT

Skip count by three to connect the dots.

This animal is the official symbol of
the Republican Party of the United States.

What is this animal? ....

Bonus Activity: Color in the drawing after connecting the dots.

Presidential
NAME SCRAMBLE

Unscramble the letters to name the four presidents on Mount Rushmore.

1. THINWAGONS ___ ___ ___ ___ □ ___ ___ ___ □ ___

2. FEJOFERNS ___ ___ ___ ___ ___ ___ ___ ___ □□

3. STOVEROLE ___ ___ ___ □ ___ ___ ___ ___ ___

4. CLONNIL ___ ___ ___ □ ___ ___ □

Unscramble the letters in the boxes to name another
place where the faces of presidents can be found.

□□ □□□□□

Barack Obama

- Barack Obama was elected president in the 2008 election. He is the 44th U.S. president. He is running for president again in 2012 as a member of the Democratic Party.

- A president is elected to a four-year term and can only serve two terms in a row.

Look through magazines and newspapers to find a photo of Barack Obama. Once you find one, color in this portrait of President Obama as accurately as possible.

Bonus Activity:
Draw in the faces of President Obama's supporters.

Mitt Romney

- Mitt Romney is running for president of the United States in 2012 as a member of the Republican Party.

- He was the governor of Massachusetts from 2003 to 2007.

Look through magazines and newspapers to find a photo of Mitt Romney. Once you find one, color in this portrait of Mr. Romney as accurately as possible.

PRESIDENTIAL WORD SEARCH

WORD BANK

OBAMA ROMNEY LINCOLN
WASHINGTON WHITEHOUSE SEAL
GOVERNMENT STRIPES
ELECTION FLAG
BRANCH STARS

The Secret Service can't get the word bank open. Help them out by finding the locked up words below.

```
S E P I R T S Y N T O D T P A
O R G G E L I N C O L N R T T
C T N E A A M N Y A E T A O A
M N T M O L A E S M E S P P A
A O A E U N A T N E T A E R C
N B D U A E B R A N C H A P S
O C W E U S E A J P E R C M D
T J X D E V E N S R T G E A E
G D I E O R E R P E A P O E L
N G L G C S F A E L T I E R E
I A R N E T T O F K P A K D C
H D I N G A A T H E R S G N T
S N M C A R O M N E Y U R A I
A O U N T S Y T H A F O D C O
W H I T E H O U S E S A E I N
```

The presidential election is determined by electoral votes. Each state's population determines its number of electoral votes. When a candidate wins the vote in a state, he wins all of the electoral votes for that state. The candidate with the most electoral votes wins.

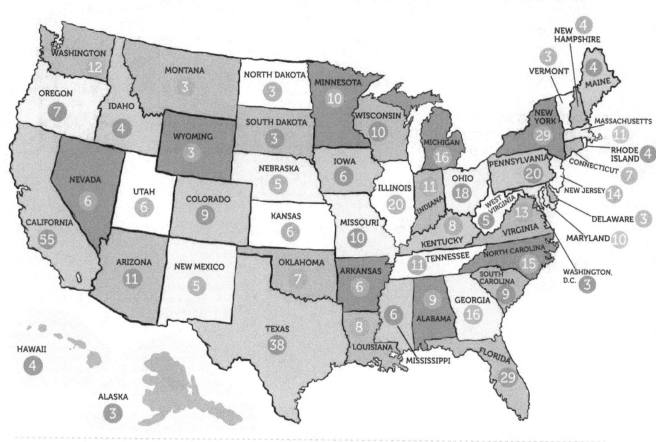

Using the map, solve the equations:

Example: North Carolina + Missouri: 15 + 10 = 25

Virginia + Ohio

Minnesota + Utah

Florida + Georgia + Alabama

Maine + Hawaii + New Mexico

Washington + Michigan + Maryland

Pennsylvania + New Hampshire + Iowa

Presidential
PAPER • DOLLS

What would you look like if you were the president?

We've all dreamed of being president at one time or another. Now, here is your chance to see what you would look like as the leader of the free world.

Color in the illustration below, then color, cut out and paste on the features and accessories that best represent you as president!

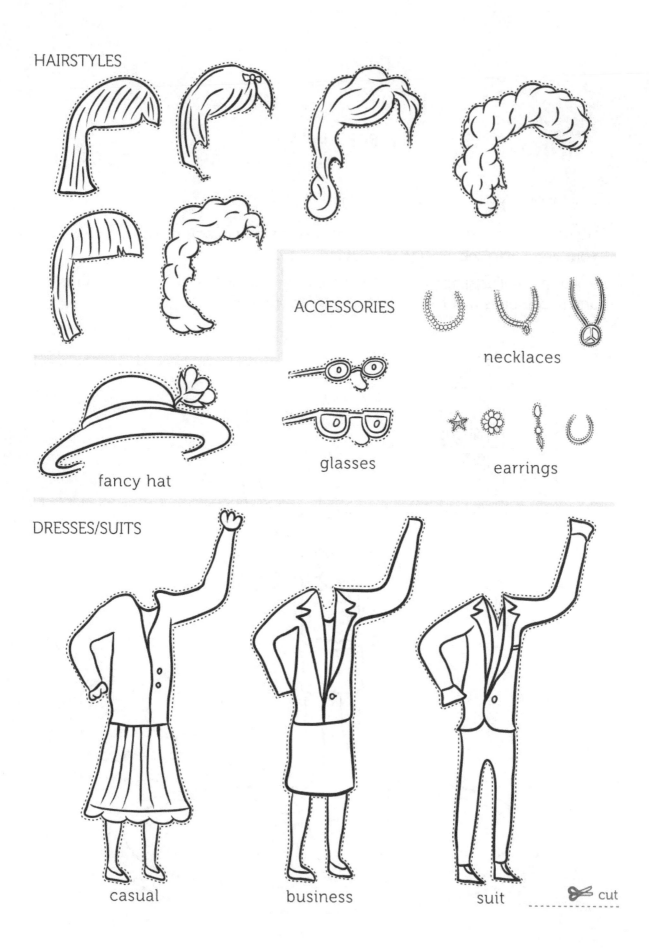

HAIRSTYLES

ACCESSORIES

necklaces

glasses

earrings

fancy hat

DRESSES/SUITS

casual

business

suit

✂ cut

PAPER • DOLLS

What would you look like if you were the president?

We've all dreamed of being president at one time or another. Now, here is your chance to see what you would look like as the leader of the free world.

Color in the illustration below, then color, cut out and paste on the features and accessories that best represent you as president!

HAIRSTYLES

SUITS

fancy

regular

casual

FACIAL HAIR

Lincoln Beard

ACCESSORIES

Lincoln Hat

Watches

Glasses

✂ cut

If I Were President...

What would you do if you became president of the United States? Write it down.

PRESIDENTIAL QUIZ

What have you learned in this presidential workbook?
Take this quiz to find out how much you know!

1 Who was the first U.S. president?

----------------------- -----------------------

2 Who is the current president?

----------------------------- ---------------------

3 The White House is in what city?

------------------------- ----------------

4 Why does the U.S. flag have 13 stripes and 50 stars?

----

5 The election is determined by what type of votes?

----

6 Match each government building with the branch of government that works in it.

The White House

• Legislative Branch

The Supreme Court

• Executive Branch

• Judicial Branch

The Capitol Building

More From Author

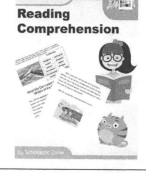

Thank You

We Welcome Your Feedback.

Feel free to get in touch with us for any feedback or questions.